C000126476

Murder & Crime

LINCOLNSHIRE

Murder & Crime

LINCOLNSHIRE

DOUGLAS WYNN

First published 2009

The History Press
The Mill, Brimscombe Port
Stroud, Gloucestershire, GL5 2QG
www.thehistorypress.co.uk

© Douglas Wynn, 2009

The right of Douglas Wynn to be identified as the Author
of this work has been asserted in accordance with the
Copyrights, Designs and Patents Act 1988.

All rights reserved. No part of this book may be reprinted
or reproduced or utilised in any form or by any electronic,
mechanical or other means, now known or hereafter invented,
including photocopying and recording, or in any information
storage or retrieval system, without the permission in writing
from the Publishers.

British Library Cataloguing in Publication Data.
A catalogue record for this book is available from the British Library.

ISBN 978 0 7524 4864 0

Printed in Great Britain

Contents

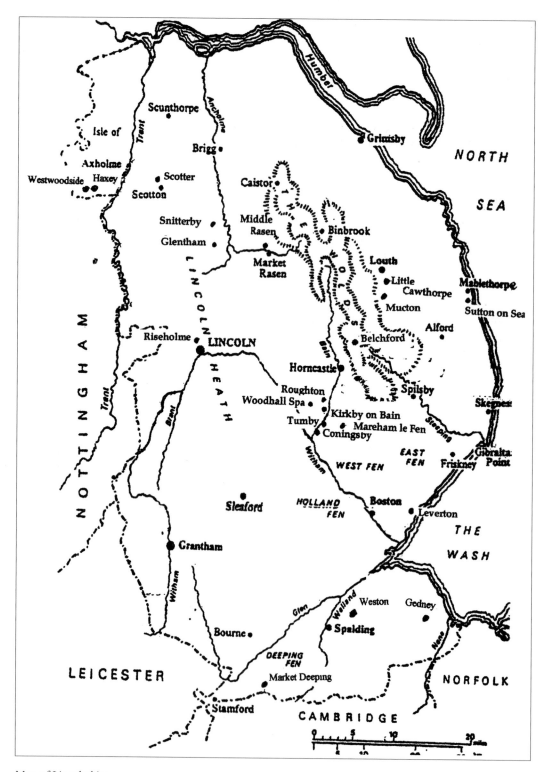

Map of Lincolnshire.

Acknowledgements

I should like to thank the staff at the Lincoln Central Library and the Grimsby Central Library for their kind assistance. My thanks are also due to David Robinson for helpful discussions, and to Stuart Sizer for loaning me a picture from his collection. Also to Mrs Mollie Twigg and Mr Alfred Bontoft for the loan of pictures and to the North East Lincolnshire Council Library Service for images and permission to use them in the book. Thanks also to the North Lincolnshire Museums Service for illustrations from their archives and permission to use them, and to the editors of the *Grimsby Telegraph* and the *Louth Leader* for permission to use part of the publications under their control. I should particularly like to thank Nicola Guy of The History Press for all her help during the writing of this book. Last but by no means least, my grateful thanks to Rosemary for help with the research, with driving, and for her constant support.

INTRODUCTION

A Short History of Lincolnshire

The area now known as Lincolnshire was occupied in pre-Roman times by the Corieltauvi tribe, but when the Romans came in AD 25 the tribe fought against them and hostilities went on for forty or fifty years. But the Romans brought considerable benefits to the area. They built dykes and waterways, notably the Foss Dyke running from the River Witham at Lincoln to the Trent at Torksey, established dry walkways across the fens, and constructed roads. They built many roads in the area and some which passed through, such as Ermine Street from London to York, and the Fosse Way from Lincoln to Exeter. They also erected as many as sixteen forts in the area and established many towns such as Lincoln itself, Caistor, Horncastle, Sleaford and Ancaster.

The Romans left in between AD 403 and AD 430, and were followed gradually by invasions of the Anglo-Saxons and the Danes. The ancient kingdom of Lindsey was established by the Angles and later became part of a larger kingdom called Mercia. This was then taken over by the Danes whose raiding army landed in East Anglia in AD 865. The Danes were followed by the Vikings and both of these left their mark in many place names, for example those ending in 'by' or 'thorpe'. And in the tenth century the shire of Lincolnshire was established. But the hierarchy of these people was destroyed by the invading Normans. William the Conqueror built Lincoln Castle and one at Tattershall, and divided the land among his followers.

During the Middle Ages, Lincolnshire, because of its large size and the availability of land, became one of the most densely populated areas in England and most of its output was agricultural. By the thirteenth century the main produce was wool and most of it was exported from Boston. Towns became rich off the backs of the sheep and built imposing churches such as those at Louth, Stamford and Boston. But a heavy tax was placed on the export of wool and the trade declined. A bridge was built over the Trent at Newark and the main route to the north which used to go through Lincoln now bypassed the town and went through Grantham and Newark instead. To a certain extent this isolated the town and the county and led to a further depression.

The Lincolnshire Rising of 1536 was one of the rebellions against Henry VIII. The King's suppression of the monasteries among other things caused resentment in Lincolnshire and beginning in Louth, Horncastle and Caistor a small army was raised. But the King brought troops up to Nottingham and Huntingdon and threatened to invade and lay waste to the county. The rebellion petered out and the leaders were hanged in London and elsewhere. During the Civil War, Lincolnshire was largely allied to the Parliamentarians, with the Royalists to the west at Newark and Belvoir Castle, but there were no great battles fought in the county and the opinions of the population in the main seemed equally divided.

The hundred years between 1750 and 1850 saw great changes in Lincolnshire's history. John Wesley had been born at Epworth in 1703 and was responsible for the rise of Methodism. Turnpike roads, canals and railways were built and agriculture expanded until Lincolnshire became one of the foremost agricultural counties in England. But as mechanization on farms increased and the demand for labour decreased there was opposition from farm labourers. Haystacks and barns were burnt, and gangs of men roamed the area trying to intimidate the farmers. The gangs seemed to operate under the leadership of a man called Captain Swing. Probably he was a mythical figure like Ned Ludd of the Luddites, but it led to a good deal of unrest for a period in the county.

Population growth was slow in the latter part of the nineteenth century and was confined largely to the towns and on the coast where seaside resorts such as Cleethorpes, Mablethorpe and Skegness began to flourish. A depression occurred in agriculture in the 1870s and the county was slow to recover from it. The First and Second World Wars helped as home-grown food became a necessity, and during the Second World War the number of RAF bases in the county increased to forty-six and the county became known as Bomber County.

Early Crime in Lincolnshire

It has been said that murder is of its time. This means that the causes of the crime vary with the era in which it is perpetrated. The morals and social opinions of the people of the time play an important part in the reasons why murder is committed. Thus the feelings of people against illegitimacy, for example, in Victorian times caused many illegitimate children to be murdered and many men to murder women who had become pregnant by them outside marriage. On the other hand it was relatively easy for some people to get away with murder.

Around 1613 a wealthy young man called Francis Cartwright had a dispute with the Reverend William Storr, the vicar of Market Rasen. At the time wealthy landowners often fell out with the clergy over the payment of tithes. This time Cartwright attacked the priest with his sword and inflicted such terrible injuries that the poor man died of his wounds. Cartwright fled to France, but because he had distinguished himself as a soldier in Holland, the king gave him a free pardon and he returned to England. But his ungovernable temper got the better of him again and he killed a man in Grantham after a quarrel. This time he was imprisoned for a year.

Contrast this with Petty Treason. This was to murder someone to whom one owed an allegiance. Like a servant murdering his master, an official murdering a higher official, or a woman murdering her husband. The penalty for this was greater than for ordinary murder and involved being burned at a stake. In July 1722 Eleanor Elsom was burned at the stake in Lincoln for murdering her husband. This horrific punishment took place with the prisoner first being coated with tar and then made to stand upon a tar barrel. A noose was placed round her neck and she was secured to the stake with iron bands. Then the barrel was removed. At this stage a kind executioner would then lean on the victim so that she was strangled before the fire was lit. Then the conflagration would be fierce because of all the tar and would become a great spectacle for the watching crowds, for this was always done in public. Luckily we don't have barbaric punishments like that today.

This book is filled with more recent murders. But it will be seen that the principal of murder being of its time still applies. There are of course many and varied reasons for the crime, and in this book I have tried to examine some of them. I hope the reader finds them as intriguing as I do.

I

Passion and Poison

'Read these!' shouted the woman and she thrust across the doctor's desk two small folded sheets. Her face was red and she looked extremely agitated. She was a small, middle aged woman with dark hair pulled back in a bun. She wore glasses and had a pinched face with an expression of anger.

Dr Armour looked across at her in some alarm. 'Calm yourself Mrs Major and tell me what this is all about.' said the doctor.

'Read those letters! Then you'll see what it's all about, why I've been so ill these past few weeks!'

She did indeed look ill and harassed and the doctor gazed across at her with sympathy, then he looked down at the sheets on his desk, picked one up and started to read it. It was a love letter and began, 'To my dearest sweetheart.' It ended with the words, 'From your ever loving sweetheart. Rose'. And there were a number of crosses at the end indicating kisses. The other one started, 'To the dearest sweetheart in the world.' And this one ended with, 'Heaps of kisses when we meet dear, to my only sweetheart.'

The doctor looked up as he could hear Mrs Major breathing heavily on the other side of the desk. 'Where did you get these?'

Ethel Major explained jerkily that she had found the letters under the bed when her husband had gone out.

'And who do you think wrote them?'

'Why my neighbour Rose Kettleborough.'

'And you are sure that they were actually written to your husband?'

'Of course they were!' she shouted, her face getting redder and her eyes glittering. Though whether they were bright with tears Dr Armour could not say. 'He's having an affair with her!' she burst out. 'I know he is! A man like that! He's… he's not fit to live!'

Mrs Major was born Ethel Lily Brown on 6 August 1892 in a cluster of cottages at the bottom of a hill, called Muckton Bottom, which was in the parish of Little Cawthorpe, on the edge of the Wolds a few miles south of Louth. Her father was Thomas Brown, who was listed as a joiner and wheelwright, and probably worked at the nearby chalk quarry. In 1897 Thomas became a gamekeeper to Sir Henry Hawley at Tumby, which is a small village on the main road south from Horncastle to Coningsby. The whole family moved the twenty miles from Little Cawthorpe to Tumby and took up residence in a small isolated cottage just outside the village on a bend in the Skegness road.

Ethel Brown went to school first in Coningsby and then in the nearby village of Mareham le Fen. In her last year at school, 1904, she was off for several weeks having caught rheumatic fever,

Aerial view of Muckton Bottom showing the chalk quarry.

which was quite common among children in those days and could result in damage to the heart valves, the cause of so many children having a weak heart. Her progress was not spectacular at school, probably because of her illness, and she left when she was twelve and for a while stayed at home looking after the family as her mother suffered with ill health. Later she worked in a shop in Coningsby and learned dressmaking, but she then returned home and practiced as a seamstress at home.

When Ethel was twenty-two she fell in love. The object of her affections was what was sometimes referred to as a gentleman farmer. He had a substantial acreage but not in the Tumby area. He was keen on shooting and joined the shoots held on the Tumby estate. How he met Ethel is a matter of speculation, but it is likely that she helped out at the big house – Tumby Lawn – serving at dinner for the members of the shooting party and he would have noticed the pretty dark haired girl who was the daughter of the head gamekeeper. That they did meet outside the big house became clear when in June 1914, Ethel became pregnant.

Her lover did not marry Ethel. He subsequently married a wealthy farmer's daughter. Ethel was in a difficult position since her father depended for his livelihood and home on his employers and their circle of friends. An arrangement was made. Ethel duly had her baby daughter, but it was given out that it was her mother's, who at forty-six could just about have had another child before the menopause. The child was given the names Auriol Iris Tryphena Brown. But the substitution of mothers did not convince everybody. It was very difficult to keep this sort of scandal, which in those days was a serious social crime, secret in rural communities. A fact which was to have important and tragic consequences.

Ethel was still at home in January 1918 when on riding through the village of Mareham le Fen one day on her bicycle she met a soldier home on leave. He was Arthur Major and he was

The cottage at Tumby where the Brown family lived.

serving with the Manchester Regiment. They had both been at Mareham le Fen School, but Arthur had left before Ethel joined, but she knew his younger brother Herbert whom she had been to school with. She also remembered Arthur being a butcher's boy when he left school. But he left the area in 1907 and went to Manchester to join his elder brother William who was working on the railways.

Arthur was staying with his brother Herbert who still lived in Mareham le Fen and he and Ethel saw a lot of each other that leave. When next she heard of him from his brother Herbert, he had been wounded in the battle of the Somme and was in hospital in Bradford. She wrote to him and later when he had some leave they met again and discussed marriage. And when next Arthur came on leave they were married at St Mary's Church, Kirkby on Bain on 1 June 1918. After a few days honeymoon Arthur went back to France. He was severely wounded again twice but was not discharged until February 1919, by which time Ethel was six months pregnant. But Arthur could not get a job and they were forced to live with her parents, and of course Auriol, in the cramped little cottage at Tumby.

It seems surprising, but Arthur didn't find out about Auriol until much later. He came from a large family in Mareham le Fen, but they had all left the area, except Herbert, by the time Arthur married Ethel, so he never heard the rumours which must have circulated in the villages. Even so the marriage was in trouble from the start. Ethel afterwards claimed that when her son Laurence was born in May 1919, Arthur seemed to take against the boy and never gave him the love a father should. But the family rubbed along. Arthur was often out of work and then they had to go back and live with her parents. And it was during this period that Arthur began to drink heavily. It confirmed to Ethel that she had made a mistake marrying Arthur. He was an uncouth, uncaring and violent drunkard; a man she would be better off without.

The school at Mareham le Fen which Ethel attended for several years.

But in those days it was difficult for a wife to leave her husband no matter how abusive he was. She could apply to the courts for a separation allowance, but it was notoriously difficult for her to ensure that the allowance from the husband was continuously paid. In addition most jobs available to independent women, and there were very few that were, were very lowly paid. And there would be even fewer jobs open to a relatively unqualified and middle aged woman like Ethel.

Ethel's mother died in 1929 and in 1931 Tom Brown retired and went to live with Auriol in a two roomed bungalow, Primrose Cottage, in Roughton, just a mile up the road from Kirkby on Bain. And a couple of years later Ethel, Arthur and Laurence moved into a council house in Kirkby on Bain. There were sand and gravel workings just south of the village and Arthur got a job as a lorry driver with Andrew Thornley, who owned the workings.

It was soon after this that Arthur somehow heard about the illegitimate child that Ethel had had. For many men at this time it would have been a serious betrayal. Although they would look with an indulgent eye on a man's peccadilloes, a woman who indulged a man before marriage was regarded as nothing more than a slut. And most men expected that the young wife they married would be a virgin, even though they might not be themselves. It certainly rankled with Arthur, and to make matters worse Ethel refused to tell him who the father was. This meant that a marriage already teetering on the brink of disaster would now have been finally tipped over the edge.

Ethel said that Arthur began drinking even more heavily and his behaviour became even more threatening and violent. He would often return from the pub, the Ebrington Arms in Kirkby on Bain, belligerent and violent. She and Laurence would leave the house before he returned and walk the mile or so up the road to her father's cottage at Roughton. He would always leave the door open for them and there they would bed down in the living room or in one of the sheds outside. Then the following morning they would trail back to their home in Kirkby. The council house was one of two pairs of semis on the road leading out of the village towards Coningsby. They were numbered one to four starting from the village end. The Majors' address was No. 2 Council Houses. Next door at No. 1 lived the Maltbys, then at No. 3 lived the Kettleboroughs and at No. 4 the Roberts.

In April 1934 Ethel received a letter. It was anonymous and written in block capitals and addressed to 'Mrs Majar, Kirby on the Bain' And it went on:

> You are slow. Don't you know how your husband spends his weekends? He has got a nice bit of fluff now! He would be done any day at the shop if it were not for missus sticking up for him. You could get rid of him easy if you had him watched.
> From one who knows about him and Mrs -----

On the back of the letter was written:

> I hear he has now got a little 'Majar' to look after.

About a fortnight later an unsigned picture postcard arrived at No. 2 Council Houses. 'Dear A. Meet me same place same time. Baby got prize.'

This convinced Ethel that Arthur was having an affair and she tackled him about it. He of course denied it and a furious row developed. It ended with Ethel moving out of the family bedroom. A short time later on a Saturday while Arthur was having a lie-in, Ethel crept up to the bedroom. She claimed later that she found two letters on the floor beneath the bed. But it is far more likely that she went through Arthur's pockets while he was asleep.

On the Sunday night Ethel and Laurence had as usual gone to her father's cottage in Tumby to sleep. When Arthur arrived home he was so drunk that he couldn't find his front door key, so he went round the back and broke a window to get in. Ethel and Laurence came back the next morning after Arthur had gone to work. Ethel noticed the broken window and went to down the road to the public telephone and phoned the council.

As a result John Holmes, Sanitary Inspector to the Horncastle Rural District Council arrived at No. 2 Council Houses. 'What seems to be the trouble?' he asked Ethel.

'Drink and my neighbour's wife are the trouble.' And she told him about Arthur's affair and even showed him the two love letters she had found. 'Is it possible for me to be made the tenant of this house instead of my husband?' she asked slyly. Holmes scratched his head and spoke carefully.

'That can only be done if your husband consents.'

Later in May he received a letter from No. 2 Council Houses.

> Mr Holmes,
> Sir – I have decided to leave as it is unpleasant for my wife, after seeing you. I thought it best giving in my notice to-day to you.
> Yours truly, Arthur Major.

Holmes consulted the council and the notice was accepted. He wrote to Arthur and said that his tenancy would end on 11 June when he would then owe rent of 16s (80p). Four days later a furious Arthur stormed into the council offices demanding to know what the letter meant. When it was explained to him he said, 'It's my wife. She's trying get rid of me.' It was eventually

Arthur Major as a butcher's boy, holding the reins.

sorted out and the tenancy returned to Arthur and he left the building. He had only been gone a few minutes when Ethel arrived.

'Has the tenancy been transferred to me?'

'No it hasn't,' said Holmes. He showed her the letter he had received. 'Did you write this?'

'Certainly not!'

One Saturday night a few days after this Ethel knocked on the front door of Cyril Thornley. He was the son of Arthur Thornley and was employed in his father's sand and gravel business and he lived in the main street of the village. Ethel's face was flushed and she was plainly very angry. 'I want to know how much my husband earned in the past week,' she demanded.

Cyril looked at her. He was well aware that some husbands didn't tell their wives what they earned; on the other hand some handed over their wage packet unopened every week and received pocket money. But he also knew about the trouble between Arthur and Ethel. He decided to play it carefully. 'I'm afraid I'm not at liberty to tell you that Mrs Major. If you want to know I suggest you ask your husband.' This incensed Ethel and she tossed her head.

'People in the village tell me that Major is idle. I'm surprised you continue to employ such a man,' she continued. 'You ought to dismiss him!'

Cyril, stung by her violence, replied, 'He's a very good working man. My father has never had any trouble with him.' Ethel threw up her hands in disgust and stalked off.

On Monday 14 May she went to see Mr Henry Tweed, who was a solicitor in Horncastle. She produced the draft of a letter she wanted the solicitor to send. It read:

The council houses at Kirkby on Bain.

To Mrs Rose Kettleborough,
I request you to stop hiding any more letters for me and I shall not write to you any more as I don't wish to speak to you or have any more trouble with you in the future.
Final notice.
Arthur Major

The letter was duly sent and on the following Saturday, which was the Saturday before Whit Sunday (now the Spring Bank Holiday), Arthur burst into the office. He was red-faced and furious and waving the letter about. 'What do you mean by sending this letter!' he shouted. It was explained to him that it was sent on the instructions of his wife.

'I knew it! I knew it! That's it! I've had enough. I'll… I'll…' He compressed his lips, since he realised that he was in a solicitor's office. And anything he said might be taken down and used against him. He left and went straight round to the offices of the *Horncastle News* in the High Street. 'I want to put an advertisement in the paper.'

The notice finally took this form:

I, Arthur Major, of Kirkby on Bain, hereby give notice that I shall not be responsible to pay my wife's debts and she has no authority to make any statement or to give or sign any notes on my behalf.
19 May 1934.
(signed) Arthur Major.

It was arranged that the notice would go in the newspaper on 25 May.

At that time it was by no means uncommon for husbands to insert such notices, for they controlled the family finances. Most wives earned very little themselves, if anything at all, and were dependent on their husbands for money. It was only in 1918 that women received the right to vote in parliamentary elections and then it was only for women householders over thirty. In 1923 wives were given equal rights to sue for divorce on the grounds of adultery and two years later received equal rights to the guardianship of children. But it was in 1928, only six years before the events related here, that all women over twenty-one were able to vote.

For the previous three weeks or so Arthur had tried to separate himself from his wife and son. He refused to eat with them and had begun buying his own food, as indicated in the poison pen letter Ethel had received. He kept his food on a paper-covered shelf in the pantry separate to the rest of the family. Nevertheless Ethel sent her son on the Friday before Whit Saturday to the shop in the village to buy a tin of corned beef. This was for Arthur since neither Ethel nor Laurence ate the food. And later Arthur gave his son money for the purchase.

On Tuesday 22 May, the day after the Whitsun Bank Holiday, Arthur was back at work. After working a normal day he left on his bicycle at about 4.30 p.m. in the afternoon. When he reached home Ethel had strategically withdrawn upstairs to change her blouse. Arthur got his own meal which consisted of tea, bread and butter and corned beef. Laurence returned at about 5.30 p.m. and saw the remains of his father's meal on a plate in the front room. Arthur was sitting in a chair in the front room, but he had his head in his hands and the boy did not speak to him. Laurence went into the scullery to have a wash and while he was there he saw, through the scullery window, Arthur go out into the back garden and he appeared to be mending a puncture on his cycle. Suddenly he keeled over and fell to the ground and lay there, his limbs jerking. Laurence rushed out to help him. 'Mother! Mother! Father's fallen over.'

Together they got the stricken man into the front room and on to a chair. He couldn't speak but was moaning in pain and shaking uncontrollably.

'Mother do you think we ought to get a doctor?'

'No. I don't think so. He'll be all right in a little while I expect.'

But he wasn't and when Tom Brown called later that evening he insisted that a doctor be called. Dr Smith of Coningsby arrived at about 10 p.m., gave the patient some castor oil and said he would make up some medicine for him if Laurence could collect it from the surgery later. The boy did so and the next day when the doctor called Arthur was a lot better, but he was still having the occasional muscular spasms and the doctor suggested that Arthur stay in bed that day.

Later that afternoon Sergeant Mitchell of the Lincolnshire Police arrived and knocked on the back door. Ethel answered the door.

'Is Mr Major home from work yet?'

'My husband is ill in bed.'

The sergeant looked surprised. 'I'm very sorry to hear that. What's the matter with him?'

'You'd better come in.' She led the way into the lounge and offered the sergeant a seat. 'He's had a fit. Well a series of fits. He was taken ill on Tuesday night.' She shook her head. 'He won't get better and drive the lorry again.'

That evening Canon Felix Blakiston, rector of Kirkby, who lived just across the road from the Majors, came to hear how Arthur was progressing and to say a short prayer for his speedy return to health. The next morning Arthur continued to improve but stayed in bed after the doctor had been. Later that evening Laurence took his father a glass of water and left it on the bedside table. Later still he saw that it had nearly all been drunk.

Another view of the council houses showing the back gardens with no fences between them.

At about ten o'clock that night he went upstairs with his mother to see Arthur. Shortly afterwards his father said he was going to have another fit. He began breathing heavily and his limbs started jerking. 'Don't leave me!' he panted. 'You have been good to me. Don't leave me! I'm going to die!'. The convulsions became stronger and he was frothing at the mouth. His head jerked back and his arms jerked up. Then his face went dark and quite suddenly he stopped breathing and his arms fell back across his chest.

The next morning, Friday, Ethel got Laurence up early, gave him a piece of paper from the pantry shelves and told him to take it and burn it at the end of the garden. When he returned, Tom Brown was there and Ethel was telling him that the notice Arthur had inserted in the paper was due to appear today. Tom sat down and wrote a short note cancelling the notice, as the person who inserted was now dead. He told Laurence to take it to the newspaper offices in Horncastle. The boy went off on his bicycle and Ethel rode her cycle to Coningsby.

When she got in to see Dr Smith at just before 10 a.m. she said, 'Major had another fit in the night and died.'

Dr Smith frowned. 'Why didn't you send for me? I might have been able to do something.' Ethel shrugged her shoulders.

'It all happened so quickly. I didn't have time to send for you. I gave him a cup of water. He drank about half, then had a fit and died.'

Dr Smith took up his pen. 'You did say that your husband had suffered fits before?'

'Oh yes. He's had them for years.'

Dr Smith wrote on the death certificate as cause of death 'status epilepticus'. Ethel took the certificate and rode back up the road to Kirkby on Bain. On the way she saw Canon Blakiston and asked him if the funeral could be the next day.

The Ebrington Arms at Kirkby on Bain where Arthur did his drinking.

'Saturday? That's a bit sudden isn't it? In any case I have a lot of commitments tomorrow.'

'Sunday then.'

After thinking about it the rector reluctantly agreed that it could be Sunday, but not until 3.30 p.m.

At just before three o'clock on the Sunday afternoon, with all the guests attending the funeral grouped in and around the Major home, two policemen knocked on the front door. They were Sergeant Mitchell of Coningsby and Inspector Dodson of Louth. When Ethel opened the front door the inspector stepped forward. 'I'm afraid the funeral must be stopped.'

'What! But you can't do that! I've invited all these people. I've made sandwiches. I've bought a seed cake. The hearse will be here in a minute!'

'I'm sorry Mrs Major. The burial must not go ahead today. The coroner has ordered a post mortem to be done on the body before it can be buried.'

The post mortem was conducted the next day by Dr Armour on the table in the scullery. He reported later that the body looked as if the man had died of asphyxia. He removed certain organs and they were sent for examination to the Home Office Analyst, Dr Roche Lynch, at St Mary's Hospital, Paddington. Inspector Dodson and Sergeant Mitchell interviewed Ethel and she made the first of several statements. They also went to Primrose Cottage and in Tom Brown's bedroom found an old chest. It was locked but when asked Tom Brown produced a key from a money belt he kept around his waist. In the chest the police discovered a bottle containing crystals, and the contents too were sent for analysis.

Dr Lynch found that the bottle contained crystals of pure strychnine, a very violent poison. In the 1920s and 1930s it was not unknown for gamekeepers to put down poison bait to kill foxes

The church at Kirkby on Bain.

and other animals which preyed on the game birds. Dr Lynch also found that all the organs sent to him from the post mortem done on Arthur Major contained strychnine.

Scotland Yard were called in and Chief Inspector Young and Sergeant Salisbury arrived from London. A few days later Ethel was arrested and taken to Horncastle Police Station and the next day the Scotland Yard officers made a search of No. 2 Council Houses. They found an old purse in which was an old key. It fitted the chest in Tom Brown's bedroom perfectly.

Ethel Major went on trial at Lincoln Assizes, held in Lincoln Castle, on Monday 29 October 1934. The judge was Mr Justice Charles, Mr E. O'Sullivan K.C. prosecuted and the defence was in the hands of the renowned counsel Mr Norman Birkett K.C. An important part of the prosecution case was that Arthur had received two separate doses of strychnine, one on Tuesday night and the other on Thursday. The prosecution further alleged that nobody but a madman, having suffered the agonies of the first dose, would give himself a second. Suicide was therefore ruled out. And in the case of murder there was nobody with a better opportunity for obtaining and giving the poison than Mrs Major. Norman Birkett did his best against the overwhelming evidence, but the jury were absent for only a little over an hour before bringing in a verdict of guilty. Ethel Major was sentenced to death and hanged at Hull Prison on 19 December 1934. She became the first woman to be executed in Britain for eight years and it caused a national sensation.

Today of course Ethel Major would not have been hanged. The charge could well have been reduced to manslaughter because of diminished responsibility, which would have attracted a lower sentence than a murder conviction. But had it not been for two factors there might never have been any charge at all. Those two factors were the location of the murder and a dog.

Herbert Maltby lived next door to the Majors at No. 1 Council Houses and he had two dogs, one a brindle and the other black and white. On the morning after Arthur had his first attack, Mrs Roberts from No. 4 was out in her back garden feeding her chickens, when she saw the black and white dog come out into the back garden. The gardens had no fences between them and it was perfectly possible for the dog to run over into the Major garden, which it did. It was also possible for Mrs Roberts to see exactly what went on. Ethel came out into her back garden and scraped something off a plate on to the ground for the dog to eat. Then she laughed and went back into the house. This astounded Mrs Roberts for she knew that Ethel hated the dog. In fact she had been known to throw a tin bath at it. And when later the dog was taken ill and died in convulsions the next day, someone put two and two together and wrote an anonymous letter to the coroner. The police investigated and dug up the remains of Herbert Maltby's dog and sent its organs off for analysis. They were full of strychnine. And the rest is history.

2

Market Day Murder

It was Wednesday 20 June 1900. A market day in Boston and Sheriff Taylor – that was his actual name, Sheriff, a common Christian name in his family – was getting a bit hot and bothered. He'd been at his market stall nearly all day surrounded by crowds of people, with the Angel Hotel and the Rum Puncheon just behind him to provide liquid refreshment if he needed it. To his left the line of stalls backed on to the railings of St Botolph's Church which jutted out into the market place. And if he had cared to look up he would have seen the statue of Herbert Ingram standing on its tall plinth in the church grounds. He would of course have seen the statue hundreds of times before but he would not have realised the significance of the man it depicted to his own situation and what was to happen to him.

Herbert Ingram was born in Boston on 27 May 1811 and educated at Loughton's Charity School and the Public School in Wormgate, Boston. He was apprenticed to a local printer, but when he was twenty-one moved to London as a journeyman printer and then in 1834 he went into partnership with his brother-in-law Nathaniel Cooke in Nottingham as a printer, bookseller and newsagent. The business prospered and they looked around for further business ventures. Herbert had noticed that newspapers included very few illustrations, but those that did sold better than those that didn't. And he reasoned that a newspaper with a lot of illustrations in it would do well. It was the birth of pictorial journalism. He and his partner moved to London in 1842 and started the *Illustrated London News*. It was an immediate success and in 1855 at Christmas it published the world's first colour supplement. Herbert Ingram became a wealthy man but he didn't forget the town of his birth. In 1856 he became Member of Parliament for Boston and was instrumental in bringing to Boston its first supply of piped water. And this is what the statue in the church yard commemorates. But the circumstance which connects Herbert Ingram with Sheriff Taylor concerns the original intention of the *Illustrated London News*, which was to make it a weekly record of crime, before they were persuaded to make it more general in character.

Sheriff Taylor was thirty years of age. He had been born in Boston, the son of Mr Sheriff Taylor, a well respected farmer in the area. By all accounts the son took after his father. He was sober, steady and industrious and had become a well-known farmer and potato dealer. He had an imposing home, Washdyke House, on the Freiston Road and a year or two before had been elected to the parish council. That year, 1900, he had become a parish constable. It was not a popular job; an unpaid, part time, often dangerous occupation and the constables worked extremely unsociable hours. But responsible citizens were expected to serve their time as parish

The Ingram statue in Boston market place.

Boston market place as it is today.

constables and so it was with Sheriff Taylor. He had married Rose Marshall in 1892 and they had had five children. One died but in 1900 they had four still alive. The eldest, Sheriff, was six, Alice was five, Clara three and baby George was eighteen months. Rose's mother and father lived in retirement just down the road from them.

Sheriff Taylor was a short man with a short temper. He was hot and not in the best of moods when he reached home that market day at about 4.30 p.m. and found that the house was empty. The three eldest children had gone to school and Rose had taken the baby with her to go into Boston to buy them some fish for their tea, but she had not yet returned. This made Sheriff extremely angry and he locked the door, put the key in his pocket and went into the yard to milk the cow. When Rose came back home she found him sullen but still angry. When she asked him for the key he refused to give it to her and when she asked him to unlock the door for her he said she must wait until he was ready.

But Rose who had a good deal of spirit herself would not be put off. 'I've got this child to see to and three more coming soon to expect their tea. I can't be doing with you and your tempers.'

And a furious row broke out between them in the yard, witnessed by a farm employee called Yates. Tempers escalated on both sides. And it culminated with Rose racing over to the kitchen window and smashing it with a stone so she could unlock the door. This further incensed Taylor and he dashed up to her, grabbed her by the shoulder, spun her round and smashed her in the face with his fist. Rose staggered back with blood coming from her nose and screaming and crying she rushed out on to the road. She met her father who had been to collect the children from school. There had been a thunderstorm earlier and the clouds were building up

Contemporary view of Freiston Road where the Taylor family lived.

again. The old man was anxious to get the children home before the storm broke. It was also an important day for the children and family for it was the first day that little Clara had gone to school.

Thomas Marshall was surprised to see his daughter rush up the road with blood streaming from her nose, coughing and spluttering. But she was plainly in a temper as well. 'That's it!' she shouted. 'I've had enough. I'll not live with that bully any longer! I'll take the children to his mother's place. She can look after them. I'll... I'll go into the workhouse rather than go back to him!'

This might seem a strange thing for a woman to say, but in those days women had very few rights. Wives were dependant on their husbands for all their money, even if they had money of their own. And a woman unsupported by her husband might have no money at all.

Thomas Marshall took out his handkerchief and wiped his daughter's face as he had done when she was a child. 'There, there, my dear. Calm yourself. Think of your children. They need you. You can't just parcel them off. No matter how you feel now, your duty is to them.'

Eventually he was able to pacify her. But it took some persuading to get her to return to her husband's house. And he had to agree to accompany her there. By the time they reached Washdyke House Taylor had opened up and was inside. He began cursing at his wife the moment she entered the door and Thomas Marshall was in two minds whether or not to go and remonstrate with him. But he decided that it might make things worse so he went back to the road. But he could still hear the bad language being shouted by Taylor as he went up the road towards his own house. And this persuaded him that someone ought to go back to Washdyke House just to make sure that everything would eventually be calmed down. And he felt that his wife was in a better position to do this than himself, for he knew that Taylor had a certain regard for her. He therefore asked his wife when he got home to go back and use her influence

TERRIBLE TRAGEDY AT BOSTON.

WIFE AND CHILD MURDERED.

THE MURDERER COMMITS SUICIDE.

A terrible tragedy was committed at Boston, on Wednesday, when a farmer named Sheriff Taylor, living on Freiston-road, murdered his wife and child, and made an attempt on his own life. Taylor who farms about 40 acres, is in comfortable circumstances, but it is known there have been frequent quarrels between himself and wife. He attended Boston market on Wednesday, and returned home about four o'clock, and after milking the cows went into the house to tea. A boy, named Yates, heard angry words pass between Taylor and his wife. Mrs. Taylor went into the yard and sent Yates to fetch her mother, who lived a short distance down the lane. At five o'clock a neighbour named Crawford, heard three shots, and saw two of Taylor's children running down the yard to meet their grandmother. On entering the house Mrs. Taylor and her three year-old daughter were found lying dead in the pantry, and Taylor was lying in a pool of blood on the kitchen floor. The upper part of Mrs. Taylor's head was blown clean off, and the child's head and face were completely shattered. The house presented a horrible spectacle, rendered all the more so by the fact that an 18 months' old child was seated in a high chair at the table, and witnessed the tragedy. Taylor used a double barrelled breech-loading gun, and having expended both barrels on his wife and child, deliberately reloaded both barrels and discharged one on himself. He appears to have placed the gun under his chin, and one side of his face is blown completely away.

Taylor was 30 years of age, and his wife about a year younger. They had been married about eight years, and had four chidren.

The tragedy caused a sensation in the neighbourhood, where the parties are well known. The inquest was held on Thursday morning.

The verdict was "That Rose Elizabeth Taylor and Clara were wilfully murdered by Sheriff Taylor at Washdyke House, Skirbeck on 20th June, 1900."

The murderer died the same evening, and at the inquest a verdict of suicide while temporarily insane was returned.

Report from the *Louth and Lincolnshire News* for Saturday 23 June 1900.

The Wellington Inn on Freiston Road where the inquest was held, as it is today.

on the two and try and make peace between them. But Mrs Marshall was not inclined to do so. 'I don't like to interfere between man and wife. I don't want them to think I'm an old interfering mother-in-law.'

This was the situation until farm hand Yates rushed into the house. 'Please ma-am will you come? Your daughter has asked me to tell you. She was scared of master and came out into the yard and asked me to fetch you quick!'

'Oh, My God!' said Mrs Marshall, appalled, and she quickly left the house and started down the road.

But she was too late. She was met by the two children, Sheriff and Alice, who came screaming up the road towards her. 'Dada has shot Mamma and Clara!'

A fearful sight met her eyes as she came into the kitchen. The room was in a shambles with chairs knocked over kitchen utensils thrown about and blood all over the walls and floor. Just by the door she stumbled across the body of Taylor who was lying on the floor moaning, his head and face a mass of blood. By the entrance to the pantry lay the dead body of poor little Clara with her face and head shattered by a shotgun blast. And in the pantry lay Rose. She too had been shot in the head and was dead. But surprisingly at the other end of the long kitchen table which was still upright was young George, unharmed and sitting in his high chair near the chimney corner, but screaming in terror.

It was afterwards surmised that Clara had been sitting at the other end of the table nearest the pantry. Taylor had aimed his gun at Rose who was standing in the pantry doorway. But the shot had missed her and hit Clara who was knocked off her stool on to the floor. Then he had fired the other barrel of the shot gun and hit his wife who collapsed into the pantry. Then he had reloaded the shotgun with two more cartridges, placed the barrel underneath his chin and fired.

But because he was a short man to get the long barrel of the shotgun beneath his chin he had to tilt his head back. Consequently the blast largely missed his brain, which would have killed him instantly, and merely destroyed his face.

Mrs Marshall raised the alarm, although neighbours had already heard the three shots and many had come running. The police were summoned and they called in Dr Reginald Tuxford. The bodies of Rose and little Clara were removed to an outhouse and Taylor who was still alive was placed on a sofa in the kitchen and afterwards removed to his bed. There was little that the doctor could do for the injured man and Taylor died in agony at about nine o'clock that night.

The inquests on the three deceased were held the following morning at the Wellington Inn. After the witnesses had been heard, the jury of thirteen men returned a verdict of willful murder against Sheriff Taylor, who the jury found committed suicide while in a state of temporary insanity. But one of the many tragedies associated with this dreadful business must be that of Thomas Marshall, who must have gone to his grave with the knowledge that if he hadn't persuaded his daughter to go back home, he might have saved her life and that of little Clara.

3

The Clue of the Salmon Sandwiches

More than eighty people attended the funeral. After the service close relatives and friends went back to Trenhorne Farm, which was in the small village of Trenhorne in eastern Cornwall. And there Mrs Hearn served them a meal. As she was going back and forwards with plates, Percy Parsons, who was the brother of the woman whose funeral they had just attended, said, 'Excuse me but are you the lady who went on the trip to Bude with my sister?'

'Yes,' said Mrs Hearn cautiously.

Percy nodded his head as if this confirmed what he had already heard. 'Where did you have the food I understand was eaten on the trip?'

But Mrs Hearn was not deceived and as if she knew what was coming she answered in an offhand way. 'Oh it was at some restaurant or café. I've forgotten the name of it now.'

'And what did you have to eat?'

'Tea, cakes, bread and butter and sandwiches.'

Percy Parson's wife now took up the questioning. 'And where did the sandwiches come from?'

Mrs Hearn could feel the tension rising in the room which had suddenly gone quiet. But she answered quite calmly. 'We took them with us.'

At this point Mrs Thomas, the mother-in-law of the dead woman, came into the room. Percy Parsons turned to her. It was obvious by now that he and his wife knew a great deal more about the business than they were letting on when he asked her, 'And did you make up the sandwiches you took with you?'

'No. Certainly not. Mrs Hearn made the sandwiches and brought them with her.'

'I understand,' persisted Parsons, 'that the sandwiches contained tinned salmon? Where did you get it Mrs Hearn?'

'From Shuker and Reed's.' Then she turned and left the room. As she was going out of the door she heard Parsons say,

'This is a very serious business, to do with my sister's death, and it must be looked into.'

Mrs Hearn was born Sarah Ann Everard on 2 June 1885 at Middle Rasen. Her father Robert Everard was basically a farm worker and had been born in Leverton near Boston. But he had had various jobs over the years including a farm servant, a carter, shopkeeper, and for a short period was a member of the Lincolnshire Constabulary. And he was constantly moving around the county. Sarah Ann, her family always called her Annie, had five homes in eight years and four schools. This could only have had an unsettling effect on the young

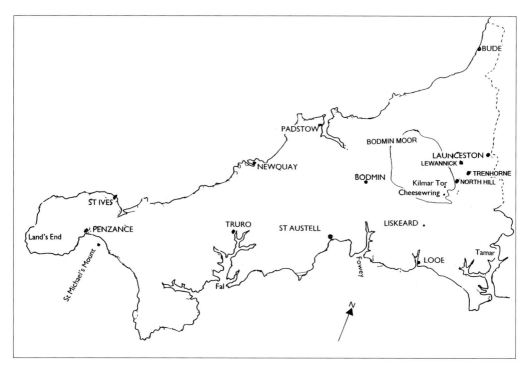

Map of Cornwall.

child, making it difficult for her to find and keep friendships outside her family, which was a large one. This may explain why in later life she often made her home with the female members of it.

When she left Welholme School in Grimsby in 1899 she went to live with her elder sister Bessie who had a dressmaking business in Sutton on Sea and after a number of years there she joined her aunt Miss Mary Everard, to help her run a cookery school in Harrogate. It was at 46 Harlow Moor Drive, then on the outskirts of the town, and across the road was the moor which led down to the Valley Gardens of Harrogate. This was a popular place for walkers and families and it was there, according to her later account of her life, that she met a young soldier.

It was in the summer of 1917. He told her that his name was Leonard Hearn and that he had been a medical student in Australia, but had subsequently joined the army and had been posted overseas. They corresponded when he went back into service and eventually he asked her to marry him. At this time, at Harlow Moor Drive, Annie was also helping to look after her elder sister Lydia, always known to the family as Minnie. Minnie had suffered some debilitating form of stomach trouble for years and needed a great deal of attention and Annie thought that having a home of her own she would be able more easily to look after her. She agreed to the proposal and she and Leonard were married in London. Then Leonard dropped his bombshell. He wanted to go back to Australia, but he wouldn't take Minnie. After several rows they agreed to part. But then, according to Annie, Leonard agreed to put an advertisement in the paper announcing his death, so that she would be able to proclaim herself a widow. Consequently two announcements were placed in the Harrogate Herald on the same day, 25 June 1919, the first announcing the marriage and the second

Welholme School in Grimsby as it is today.

announcing the death of Leonard Wilmot Hearn M.D. And thereafter Annie always called herself Mrs Hearn.

In November 1919 Mrs Hearn and Minnie moved to Weston-Super-Mare, hoping that the sea air would help Minnie's illness. But in 1921 they moved again, this time to the village of North Hill, south of Launceston in Cornwall. They were both very poor. Mrs Hearn made a precarious living baking cakes and pastries and displaying them in the window of the little cottage. But then she discovered she could claim more money from Poor Relief by looking after an old and infirm old lady. They moved again, renting a larger house in the small hamlet of Trenhorne a mile or two to the north.

Trenhorne House was a large property split into two flats and Mrs Hearn rented one half of it. Trenhorne is a very small place and she soon got to know most of the inhabitants. William and Alice Thomas owned Trenhorne Farm and William soon made it a habit to visit the two sisters, bringing them a daily paper and often fetching shopping for them when he went into Launceston, for he was one of the few people in the area who owned a car. He would often stay the evening playing cards with them for Minnie was not capable of going out much.

During the early part of 1930 Minnie began to get worse. Her doctor put her illness down to gastric catarrh, an old term for what is today called gastritis, a rather vague term covering a range of disorders from mild indigestion to a dangerous emergency. She suffered greatly and died in July of that year, being buried in the churchyard at the nearby village of Lewannick.

A few weeks after this William had his mother staying with him. She lived near Bude on the north Cornish coast and when she had decided to go back home he proposed to take her in

Contemporary picture of 46 Harlow Moor Drive in Harrogate.

the car. He suggested to his wife Alice and to Mrs Hearn that they might like to come with him for a day's outing. So one day in October they all set out on the twenty-five mile journey. They dropped William's mother off at her home and the others went on to Bude and called in at Littlejohn's café on the Strand. On the way home Alice began to be very sick. They managed to get her home and into bed and while Mrs Hearn stayed to look after her, William went for the doctor. She was still not very much better the next day and the doctor persuaded her to stay in bed. William asked Mrs Hearn if she would stay on at the farm to look after Alice and she agreed.

Alice slowly began to improve but she still wasn't well enough to get up and after about a week, William decided he'd better go and tell her mother who only lived a few miles away. Mrs Tryphena Parsons came back with William and took over most of the cooking at the farm, but Mrs Hearn stayed on. The following weekend Mrs Hearn cooked the Sunday dinner and Alice was well enough to get up for a short time. But later in the day she deteriorated, had a very disturbed night and the following day her nose started to bleed. Her mother couldn't stop it and called William in from the fields and he went for the doctor. He said that she was seriously ill and would have to be transferred to a hospital. She was taken to Plymouth Hospital and died early the next morning. But the consultant physician there was suspicious of the death and ordered a post mortem, at which certain of her organs were taken for analysis.

After the funeral of Alice Thomas, Mrs Hearn went back home. William called round to see her the next day, but her side of Trenhorne House was shut up. However the following day William received a letter from her:

Entrance to Trenhorne House several years ago.

Dear Mr Thomas,
Goodbye. I am going out if I can. I can't forget that awful man – things he said. I am innocent – innocent (both these words were underlined). But she is dead and it was my lunch she ate. I can't bear it. When I am dead they will be sure I am guilty and you at least will be clear. May your dear wife's presence guard and comfort you still.
Yours,
A.H.
My life is not a great thing anyhow now dear Minnie is gone. I should be glad if you will send my love to Bessie and tell her not to worry about me. I will be all right, my conscience is clear, so I am not afraid of afterwards.

Soon after this, Superintendent William Pill of the Launceston Division of the Cornwall Constabulary was informed by the public analyst that he had found arsenic in the organs of Mrs Thomas. And a search was begun for Mrs Hearn. It was discovered that she had gone by taxi to Looe, a seaside resort on the south coast of Cornwall and a search of the cliffs above the town unearthed a check coat like the one she had been wearing in the taxi, flung over a gorse bush.

Had she committed suicide by throwing herself off the cliffs into the sea? Opinions were divided but the search went on. By now all the newspapers had got hold of the story and it became a national sensation. Reports of sightings of Mrs Hearn came in from all over the country. The *Daily Sketch* ran a piece called 'Marriage Riddle'. They discovered that the only Dr Leonard Hearn who had ever been on the medical register was a Dr Leonard Wilfred Hearn, who at the time of the newspaper article was the Tuberculosis Officer for Nottinghamshire. And

Trenhorne Farm several years ago.

he had never heard of Dr Leonard Wilmot Hearn. The newspaper also found that there was no record of the marriage.

At the time she said the marriage took place Mrs Hearn also produced a photograph of her husband which she showed her relatives and always kept a copy by her bedside. This photograph was published in the *Daily Sketch* and it turned out to be the great grandson of the third Marques of Londonderry. His mother was greatly distressed when she saw the photograph and pointed out that her son had been in the Royal Flying Corps, but was shot down in France and died of his wounds in 1917. So he couldn't possibly have married Annie Everard in 1919.

The police search for Mrs Hearn continued and on 1 December the police issued a new description of her.

She is 45, 5ft 2ins tall, with grey eyes and brown shingled hair. She has a sallow complexion and is of medium build; is well spoken but with a North Country accent. Last seen in Looe on 10 November. She may seek employment as a cook since she has been a teacher of cookery and is known to be a good cook.

The *Daily Mail* also published a photograph of her and offered a reward of £500 (a very substantial sum for those days) for either conclusive evidence of her death or information which would enable the police to interview her.

The inquest on Alice Thomas was held in late November and the findings were that she had died of arsenic poisoning, but there was not sufficient evidence to show by whom and by what means it had been administered. After the inquest the Cornwall Police sent a full

The Strand at Bude as it looks today.

report to the Director of Public Prosecutions, including also the death of Lydia Maria Everard (Minnie), aged fifty-two. They also sent an application for the exhumation of the body. This was not unreasonable, since the symptoms of gastric catarrh can be very similar to those of arsenic poisoning. The exhumation took place in the Lewannick churchyard on 8 December. It was a foul day with snow showers in the morning, though it brightened up later in the day. The examination was made by the Plymouth pathologist who conducted his operations in the churchyard behind a screen and organs were removed for analysis.

In January 1931 a Mr Cecil Powell, an architect in Torquay, recognized the picture of Mrs Hearn he saw in the newspaper as the lady he had recently engaged as a housekeeper under the name of Faithful. He got in touch with the Torquay Police. They contacted the Cornwall Police and Sergeant Trebilcock, who knew Mrs Hearn by sight, was sent to Torquay. It was arranged with Mr Powell that he would send her out shopping and the police would pick her up outside. But she went out the back way and they missed her. Eventually they caught up with her late at night on her way back and Sgt Trebilcock recognised her by the light of a street lamp. She was arrested and taken back to Launceston police station.

Committed for trial by the Launceston magistrates she finally went on trial on Monday 15 June 1931 at the Bodmin Assizes in the Shire Hall at Bodmin before Mr Justice Roche. The prosecution was in the hands of Mr du Parcq and she was defended by Mr Norman Birkett. Mr Powell, who had received the reward offered by the *Daily Mail*, had been so impressed with her service to him during her stay that he gave the reward towards her defence.

Mrs Hearn was charged with two murders, that of Lydia Maria Everard and Alice Maud Thomas, since arsenic had been found in both bodies. Mrs Hearn, who was known by the

Contemporary view of Alice Thomas' grave.

newspapers as the silent widow, answered quietly to both charges, 'I am innocent.' She was wearing a brown costume and matching brown hat pulled down well over her eyes. She sat in the dock between a hospital nurse and a wardress and occasionally scribbled notes which she passed to her solicitor, Mr Walter West from Grimsby.

Mr du Parcq brought evidence to show that Mrs Hearn had bought a 1lb (454g) tin of Cooper's weed killer, which contained 70 per cent arsenic, in July 1926. The tin would have contained 4,000 grains of arsenic and the lethal dose was only two grains. The only other evidence of anyone having arsenic in the neighbourhood was Mr William Thomas, who kept for some years a sheep dip containing 22 per cent arsenic and two tins of worm tablets containing 14 per cent arsenic which he kept in the kitchen at the farm.

Miss Lydia Everard, said Mr du Parcq, was attended by a doctor as far back as 1922, but the first accurate account of her symptoms dated from the beginning of 1930. He said that experts believed that Miss Everard had been poisoned for as long as seven months before she died. Subsequently Mrs Hearn bought a tin of salmon on 3 September 1930 and made up sandwiches on white bread for the trip to Bude. It was then, suggested the prosecution, that Mrs Thomas received her first dose of arsenic. But it was not enough to kill her and so she was given another larger dose over the weekend just before she died. And Mrs Hearn was in a good position to give just that dose. Her flight showed her guilt and she must have had a mackintosh under the check coat she left on the cliffs at Looe to protect her in the journey on to Torquay.

But Mr Norman Birkett pointed out that the tin of Cooper's weed killer that Mrs Hearn bought contained a blue-coloured powder. If she used anything approaching a lethal dose in the sandwiches, it would have coloured the bread blue. And everyone would have noticed it.

The churchyard at Lewannick today.

Bodmin's Shire Hall where Mrs Hearn's trial took place.

And he brought forward experiments done by Sir Sydney Smith, at that time one of the foremost authorities on forensic medicine in the country, to prove that that was true. At this the prosecution case collapsed. They had contended that Mrs Hearn administered two doses, one by sandwiches and the other just before she died. But if Mrs Hearn could not be proved to have given the first in the sandwiches, there was no proof she gave any at all. For anybody who was there at the time could have administered the second. And it was known that several people gave her food or drink during that time.

The evidence against her in the case of her sister was even shakier. The soil in parts of Cornwall has quite a high concentration of arsenic in it due to the nearby presence of old lead and copper mines. This was the case in the Lewannick churchyard. Birkett suggested that since the disinterment had taken place in a snow storm, the samples could have become contaminated with soil blown by the wind. This would account for the low concentration of arsenic found in her body.

The jury had no difficulty bringing in verdicts of not guilty for both charges and Mrs Hearn walked free from the court. She made her way back to Grimsby where she had a celebratory meal at the Yarborough Hotel, with her solicitor Mr Walter West and her two brothers who still lived and worked in Grimsby. Then she boarded a train to Doncaster to stay with her sister Bessie who had given evidence on her behalf at the trial. So the story began and ended in Lincolnshire.

4

Murder in the Isle

The Isle of Axholme is in the north east part of Lincolnshire, roughly between the towns of Scunthorpe, Gainsborough and Doncaster. It is a largely flat and originally marshy area bounded by the rivers Ouse (which later becomes the Humber) to the north and the River Trent to the east. And it is the only part of Lincolnshire lying east of the River Trent. To the west is the River Don and to the south the River Idle. It is some eighteen miles from north to south and only about five or six miles from east to west, except in the north where it becomes narrower and ends in a point. The name derives from the Saxon 'Axel-holme', 'Axel' being the old name for Haxey, which at one time was the principal village, and '-holme' which was used to indicate a river island.

The two things which the area is most famous for today are Epworth, the birthplace of John Wesley, the founder of Methodism, and the Haxey Hood Game, played every year on 6 January. John Wesley was born in 1703 at Epworth rectory, the fifteenth child of the Reverend Samuel Wesley and his wife Susannah. They actually went on to have nineteen children, one of whom was Charles Wesley, born in 1708, who is said to have written 6,500 hymns of which 500 are still in use.

The Haxey Hood Game is based on an ancient legend, which may have some basis in fact. Haxey is one of the higher parts of the Isle and lies on one side of a hill, with the nearby village of Westwoodside on the other side. The story goes that in the fourteenth century the wife of the lord of the manor was riding up the hill when the wind blew off her silk riding hood. Thirteen farmhands who were working in the fields around chased the hood all over the fields until one of them caught it. But he was too shy to return it himself and so he gave it to another who did. The lady was amused and delighted by the efforts of the farm workers, but she called the one who had found it but would not hand it over a fool. The one who did hand it over, she said, had acted like a lord. And she asked her husband to give to the community thirteen acres of land, provided that the whole thing was enacted every year on the day it happened, 6 January. Whether this is all true is problematical but it is true that a land owner of the time, John De Mowbray, 3rd Baron Mowbray of Axholme, did grant land to the villagers in 1359.

Today the game is very much organised. Thirteen men every year dress themselves in red. One is designated the Fool and has a very elaborate costume with flowers in his hat and another is the Lord and he is similarly dressed. Weeks before the event they go round knocking on doors to raise money for charity and there is a parade in Haxey village before the event

Contemporary view of Westwoodside.

begins. Then men from three pubs in Haxey, and one in Westwoodside, gather on the hillside. The hood is represented by a leather cylinder and is pushed into a large scum. The object is to try and carry the hood to one or other of the four pubs, when that pub is declared the winner. The game has been played for some 650 years, making it the oldest surviving tradition in England.

But in July 1861 the hamlet of Westwoodside in the parish of Haxey was visited by a tragedy so terrible that it is remembered in the village today. George Wilson was a local farmer, well known and liked in the village. He and his wife Ann had three children, Lucy who was two and a half, William who was four and Elizabeth who was seven. Ann was regarded in the village as a rather peculiar woman who had bouts of debilitating depression and ill health, particularly so since the previous December when her fourth child was born and only lived a few weeks.

On the evening of Monday 8 July, George Wilson left the farm and told his wife that he would be back the next day. Sometime during the evening Ann went round to her next door neighbour John Webster.

'John, would you let your son take me to Wheatley tomorrow morning?'

North Wheatley, about nine miles to the south near East Retford was where Mr Parr, her father, lived.

Webster pursed his lips and looked doubtful. 'Well I don't know about that Mrs Wilson. He's rather busy tomorrow. But you can loan my pony and cart and drive yourself if you like.'

'That's kind of you John. I shall be back the next day.'

And so it was arranged. The next morning at about four o'clock – at that time of year it was light at that hour – John Webster walked past the Wilson house on his way to the paddock where he kept his pony. He noticed that it looked shut up with all the blinds drawn. At about six o'clock he was back at the Wilson house with the pony and cart. He went round the back and found the back door open as it usually was.

'Mrs Wilson,' he called.

'Come in John.' He went in the kitchen and found her washing herself in the sink.

'I shan't be long John.'

And shortly afterwards she left by herself in the pony and cart.

She arrived later that morning at her father's house in North Wheatley to be met by her brother Joseph who helped her down from the seat on the cart.

'Where have you left the children, Ann?'

'Don't worry. I've taken care of them.'

About eleven o'clock that morning George Wilson arrived at Mr Parr's house unexpectedly. He was surprised to see his wife there and took her on one side to talk to her. A few moments later Joseph heard a howl of distress from George and he rushed up to him.

'Whatever is the matter, George?'

'She's murdered my children! Oh my poor little babies!'

'What all of them?'

'She's put them all in the cistern!'

Cisterns were often large containers set into the ground to collect and store water for the farm. In effect they were shallow wells. They were usually covered with a flag stone to prevent loss by evaporation.

'Is this true?' asked Joseph of his sister.

Haxey as it looks today.

She replied tearfully, 'They are in heaven.'

The whole story eventually came out. In the early morning of that day Ann had sent the only servant who lived in the house away on an errand which would take her all day to accomplish. Then she had heaved aside the heavy flag stone. Going upstairs she first brought down the youngest, Lucy, still asleep in her arms, kissing her all the way down. Then she had dumped her in the cistern. The four year old William was more difficult, but she managed to lead the still sleepy boy down the stairs until he too could be put in the cistern. By this time Elizabeth, the seven year old, was awake and had to be enticed down the stairs and out into the back yard. But after a struggle she too was confined to the water. George was distraught and prostrated by the terrible news and had to be restrained from attacking his wife. He insisted that the police be called immediately.

The killing of children by their parents is probably as old as the human race itself. Certainly malformed babies have been dispatched in the past by races as different as the Australian Aboriginals and the Eskimos. And it has been widely used as a form of population control in poor countries such as India and China. It has been said that getting rid of children born out of wedlock was common in European countries as late as the seventeenth century. The first act making it an offence to kill an illegitimate child was passed in the reign of James I, and the offence was murder for which you could be hanged. It was not until 1938 with the first Infanticide Act that it was decreed that a mother who killed her own child, of under a year, would be charged only with manslaughter, which at that time did not carry the death penalty.

Thus Ann Wilson was in considerable danger when she was brought before the magistrates and sent to trial at Lincoln Assizes on 26 July 1861 on a charge of willful murder of her child

Contemporary view of North Wheatley.

Lucy Wilson, the only murder she was actually charged with. She presented a tragic figure as she stood in the dock, a small, feeble looking woman dressed in mourning clothes. And she had to support herself by grasping the front of the dock during the proceedings. She seldom moved her head during the examination of witnesses and kept her eyes fixed down on the barristers' table. Mr Bodene appeared for the prosecution and she was defended by Mr Stephens.

John Webster was called as a witness and he described the conversation he had with Ann on the evening before and the day of the tragedy. He also described how he was called to the Wilson house by his wife later that day. He found George Wilson in great distress and George asked him if he would help him with the bodies of his children who were still in the cistern. John Webster told him not to distress himself any further. He would see to what was necessary. He went to the cistern, which he described as a large one, and he had to get inside it to retrieve the bodies which were lying in only a couple of feet of water. They were all in their night clothes.

Next came his wife Mary Webster. She testified that she had known Ann Wilson very well for several years. For some time she had thought she was very weak in mind and body. She had been confined the previous December but the child had only lived for a few weeks. And since then she had seemed to get worse. She complained of pains in her head and she seemed very depressed. She was very kind to her children but she had heard her say, 'How much better my children would be if they were in Heaven.' And she had also told her that it would be a good thing if the little boy was in heaven, for it would be a bad thing if he grew up to be a drunkard.

Joseph Parr gave evidence. He said that in the previous April Ann had come to stay at the family home for two weeks. She seemed at that time very low in spirits. On a subsequent visit she said that she had come to say goodbye to her sisters, although they were not going anywhere. On the 19 June he was staying with his sister at Westwoodside. As they sat down to breakfast she asked him for a blessing. She then went out and came back several times and each time asked him for a blessing. In those days this might have meant that she was asking for divine protection or aid or for some sort of approval from her brother. She also told him that she wished her children were in heaven as this was such a wicked world. Joseph was much disturbed by his sister's behaviour. He later wrote to George Wilson telling him that he thought he ought to get his wife to seek medical help and that she should be watched at all times.

The doctor who had been attending Mrs Wilson was also called. He was Mr Pritchard, described as a surgeon of Stockwith, who had attended Ann in May. He said that at the time he did not think she was of sound mind. He saw her again in June and found her very depressed and melancholic. There were no drugs at that time for depression and all he could do was to advise her husband and her friends to get her to seek cheerful society as it would help to strengthen her mind.

At this stage of the trial the judge told the jury that from the evidence which had been presented it was apparent that the prisoner was not in a sane state of mind when she destroyed her children. She was labouring under a kind of religious melancholy, or a delusion equivalent to this. She considered it her duty to the Almighty that she should send her children to him and release them from the cares and troubles which she had an idea would beset them in this world. If the jury were of a similar opinion they would no doubt consider that the case ought not to be proceeded with any further. After a brief consultation the jury acquitted the prisoner on the grounds of insanity, and the judge, remarking that he thought they had arrived at the right decision, ordered that the unfortunate woman should be confined at her majesty's pleasure.

5

The Robbery that Went Wrong

The large village of Pinchbeck is only a couple of miles north of Spalding to which it is now joined. In 1879 a footpath ran from Steppingstone Lane on the north side of Spalding to a road communicating with 'Two Plank' Bridge and then on to the outskirts of Pinchbeck. It was often used by farmers and the cottagers of Mill Green, and provided an alternative route across the fields to Pinchbeck. At seven o'clock on Sunday morning, 9 November, Alfred Barratt, a butcher from Spalding used the footpath to go and look at some cattle in a field near Pennygate. He was following the footpath which crossed a carrot field when he saw someone lying among the carrot plants. He approached and saw that it was a man lying on his back with one foot drawn up under the other knee. Thinking he was asleep he kicked his foot. But the man did not move. The butcher then knelt and felt the man's leg. It was cold and stiff. He was obviously dead.

Barratt rushed back to Spalding and knocked up P.C. Archer, whom he knew lived near the police station, and the two went back to the carrot field. The policeman noticed that many of the carrot tops had been crushed and broken around the body, so there might have been a struggle in the vicinity of the body. The man was wearing cords and his belt was above the top of his trousers. The left-hand trouser pocket was cut away. But there were no signs of actual violence on the body. Two caps were found nearby and a piece of blue ribbon. And clutched in the dead man's hand was a door key.

'It looks to me like a robbery with violence,' said Archer. 'I'll just go through the rest of his pockets to see if we can identify him.'

In one pocket he found half a pound of sugar, nine bootlaces, and a spring balance. When Barratt saw the balance he exclaimed, 'Now I know who that is. It's Deaf George!'

'You're right. It's a wonder I didn't recognise him before. His name is George Rolt and he lived in Pinchbeck.'

George Rolt was about fifty when he died. He was very deaf due to an accident when he was a farm worker, but he could communicate quite well with people sometimes using a kind of sign language. He was in fact a peddler, or rag and bone merchant as they were sometimes called, and plied his trade with a horse and cart. He would buy merchandise from J.T. White's fancy emporium in Spalding and hawk it around the nearby villages. He was separated from his wife who lived in Holbeach, but she came and identified the body. She said that he was in the habit of carrying large sums of money in his pocket. He lived in a small cottage overlooking Blue Gowt Drain and had as a housekeeper a young woman of twenty-three, Elizabeth Ireland.

The Punchbowl Inn today.

The body was removed to the mortuary, or death house as it was called, in Spalding and a post mortem performed by Dr Stiles and Mr C.K. Morris, who was a surgeon. They discovered that Rolt had two broken ribs, but that he died of asphyxiation, possibly aggravated by the fact that he had a weak heart. They surmised that somebody had kneeled or sat on his chest to immobilise him while he was robbed and that the compression stopped him breathing. In 1828 Burke and Hare, the notorious body-snatchers of Edinburgh, are thought to have murdered sixteen people by this method and it became known as 'Burking'.

Superintendent Leaper of Spalding was in charge of the case and he soon began inquiries in the town. The crime had caused a sensation. The last time there had been a murder there was in 1741 when a certain Margaret Ives was done to death. Soon information began to pour into the police station. Edward Brummitt who was a blacksmith in Spalding had been to Pinchbeck on his bicycle the Saturday night of the murder and was returning along the Steppingstone Lane when he heard some people quarrelling. He recognised Rolt's voice, but there was a woman's voice he did not recognise and also another man's. He was about twenty or thirty yards away when he first heard them and he got off his bicycle, not wishing to intrude on the dispute. He heard Rolt ask for his house key, so he could go home, but he did not hear any reply to that. Then he heard him ask for it again and the female voice replied, 'You heard what he says.' Brummitt then heard Rolt reply, 'You can have someone else to go to sleep with you tonight. I don't care.' There were further confused voices after that but Brummitt could not make out what was said and then they moved off and he continued his journey.

James Lawrence, who was a hairdresser in Spalding, reported that at about 7.30 p.m. that Saturday evening George Rolt came into his shop for a shave. When he had gone and sometime

The Peacock Inn today.

later Elizabeth Ireland came in. She had on what he described as a light hood with a blue ribbon around the neck. She asked if Deaf George had been in and the barber said he had but had now left. And she left immediately.

John Ecclestone was a drover who lived in Spalding. On the Saturday night he went to the Punch Bowl public house at about seven o'clock and saw Elizabeth Ireland there. She had a young lad of twelve or thirteen sitting with her and she was talking to a man he did not know. Ecclestone left the pub after a short time and returned after about half an hour. Ireland was still talking to the other man.

The landlord of The Peacock Inn in Spalding was James Paddison and the pub was about 200 to 300 yards from Steppingstone Lane. Paddison said that he had seen Elizabeth Ireland and two men he didn't know in his pub between 7 p.m. and 8 p.m. that Saturday night. Ireland had two four-penny's worth of brandy and the two men two pints of beer. But although he didn't know the men she was with, another of his patrons knew both of them. William Boothby was a labourer who lived in Pinchbeck. He knew George Rolt well and also his housekeeper Elizabeth Ireland and he named the two men as Henry Howitt and John Vessey. Both of them he had seen working on agricultural machinery during the last summer and he had also noticed Elizabeth working with them. There was also a young boy with the woman and he knew him as William Clark. Just before they left the pub he heard the woman tell the young boy to go and wait for them at the level crossing gates on the Pinchbeck Road. Boothby and a friend left the Peacock just after Elizabeth and the two men and saw them going along Steppingstone Lane. Boothby and his friend went along the Pinchbeck Road and at the railway gates saw the young boy. He asked them if 'Betty' was coming and they said they didn't know. They continued on home.

Westlode Street today.

Superintendent Leaper now thought he had enough evidence to interview Elizabeth Ireland and he went to Rolt's house in Pinchbeck. She was next door at Mr and Mrs Clark's house when he arrived. He asked her to come to Rolt's house as he wanted to ask her some questions. During the interview she said that she was twenty-three. She came originally from Deeping St Nicholas, where her parents were still living. She had an uncle living in Spalding and she had been living in as a housekeeper to George Rolt for about a year.

But the strangest story he heard that day came from Mrs Rachel Clark. She had seen the rag and bone man that Saturday night. He had come to her house and asked if Elizabeth had left the front door key to his house with her. Apparently they only had the one key. She told him that Elizabeth had not and Rolt said he would go looking for her. Her son William often went with Ireland to Spalding to collect a paper for her husband. When William came home eventually that Saturday night he said that he had left Ireland behind. Soon after this they all went to bed. But they hadn't been in bed very long when she heard the sound of breaking glass and someone coming up the stairs. She was terrified. But then she heard a familiar voice.

'It's only me,' called Elizabeth Ireland. 'I had to break a window to get in.'

'Whatever's the matter?'

'There's two men outside my door with a knife. I heard them say, "Here she comes. Now we'll have her!" We'll all be murdered in our beds!'

Ireland appeared to be hysterical. But though Rachel and her husband looked out of the window they could see nobody outside the Rolt house. However, Mr Clark saw something white by the front door. Rachel told him she thought it was Elizabeth's white hood. She stayed all night and in the morning went back home, but came running back to say she had seen some

MURDER

AT

SPALDING.

A Man Robbed and left to Die in the Darkness.

FINDING OF THE BODY.

SCOURING THE COUNTRY FOR THE CULPRITS.

THE POLICE AT WORK.

[BY OUR OWN AND SPECIAL REPORTERS.]

One of the most appalling and sickening events it has ever been our duty to record happened at Spalding on Saturday night last. A harmless, inoffensive man, in returning to his home after market, was robbed and — if not killed outright— so seriously and fatally injured that he soon afterwards died from the effects of the injury before anyone knew of the occurrence, and whilst within a comparatively short distance of the town, his murderers

Headline from the *Lincolnshire, Boston and Spalding Free Press and South Holland Advertiser*, 11 November 1879.

49

men on the 'ramper' (the main road into Spalding) who said a man had been found dead and taken to the mortuary in Spalding. He was dressed as Rolt had been and she was sure it was him.

Later Superintendent Leaper asked her to search the house to see if anything was missing and she said that all Rolt's best clothes had gone. And a window at the rear of the premises had been broken, no doubt to effect an entry. The policeman did not believe Elizabeth's story and he arrested her, taking her down to the police station in Spalding. The superintendent then sent out descriptions of Howitt and Vessey to all police stations in the area asking for the men to be detained. Since the instructions went by telegraph, however, he had to wait until Monday because the telegraph offices were closed on Sunday.

But the inquiries soon bore fruit. P.C. Dance, who was stationed at Langrick, three or four miles to the north west of Boston, received the information on the afternoon of Monday. He knew both the men well and had seen them working in the fields and on the roads and he also knew that they often drank at the Windmill public house some four miles away. He went there, meeting P.C. Danes on the way, and when they entered the pub they saw that it was quite crowded. But in a corner by the fire sat Howitt. He had his arms on the table and his head on his arms, apparently asleep. Danes tapped him on the shoulder.

'Hullo Harry. Where do you come from?'

The man answered immediately without raising his head. '50 Welby Street, Grantham.'

The reply puzzled the policemen. And since they were in plain clothes they received curious looks from the rest of the men in the tap room. They decided to have a word with the landlady. While they were doing so, Dance noticed the man get up and rush out of the room. They quickly followed, but he had disappeared into the gathering darkness. That really should have been the end of the matter. But both policemen knew the area like the back of their hands. They knew where all the farms were and where there would be farm buildings and barns in which the fugitive might try to hide. It was a long search but eventually they found him hiding under some straw in a stable on a farm some five miles from the Windmill public house. Dance put the cuffs on him and took him in a cart to Boston, where he handed him over to Superintendent Sowden. Howitt stayed the night in the cells at Boston and the next day P.C. Archer came and took the prisoner back to Spalding.

When he was seen by the superintendent that evening he was anxious to make a statement. But the policeman told him to sleep on it and he would take the deposition in the morning. Then Howitt made his statement. In it he said that he and Vessey (he called him Jack) had stayed for ten days at the Butchers' Arms which was at 61 Westlode Street Spalding. On the Saturday evening they were having their tea there when Elizabeth Ireland came in with a young boy. They chatted for a bit and they asked her to meet them in the Still public house. She refused, but later they saw her coming out of a baker's shop and together they all went into the Punch Bowl and then the Peacock. When they left the pub she sent the boy up to the railway gates to wait for them. Then they met Rolt on Steppingstone Lane. He demanded his house key from Elizabeth Ireland. At first she refused, but then gave it to him and he went back towards Pinchbeck. She told them that he carried a lot of money in his left-hand trouser pocket and if they would take it she would go with them to London or anywhere they liked. They caught up with Rolt and held him down while she cut off his pocket and robbed him. Then all three went up to his house. Jack and he waited outside while Elizabeth went inside and brought him a hat to replace the one he had dropped in the field. She then said she would go and pack and they would catch the mail train to London. But she never came back. Howitt fell into the Blue Gowt Drain, so they broke into the house to get him some dry clothes and took some other clothes to pawn. He never meant to kill the old man.

After the completion of the crime the two men left Spalding, travelling first to Weston and Holbeach and then back through Fosdyke to Boston. When the description of the two wanted men came from Spalding a search was made in Boston and Vessey was found to be staying at the Flying Dutchman in Rosegarth Street. A couple of Boston police sergeants arrested him there and he was taken to the police station to await an officer from Spalding. When the officer arrived he did not recognise Vessey from the description he had been given and said that it was not the man he wanted. And Vessey, to the chagrin of the Boston police, was released. But a fuller description was soon issued from Spalding and Vessey was eventually located on a farm at Frithville, near Sibsey, north of Boston. He was arrested there and taken back to Spalding.

Elizabeth Ireland (twenty-three), Henry Howitt (twenty-five) and John Brewster Vessey (twenty-two) went on trial at the Lincoln Assizes on Friday 30 January 1880, before Sir James Fitzjames Stephen on a charge of murder. Mr J.G. Lawrance and Mr Ewen Bennett prosecuted and the prisoners were defended by the Hon. E. Chandos Leigh. The prosecution case was strong. Apart from the confession of Howitt and the evidence of witnesses, a boot mark made at the scene of the crime matched one of Howitt's boots and of the two caps found one was identified as his. The trial took ten hours and the jury retired late in the evening. They took only twenty minutes to bring in guilty verdicts against all three. And the judge sentenced all three to death. But in view of the comparative youth of the prisoners and the fact that George Rolt had a weak heart, which may have contributed to his death, it was not surprising that all three were reprieved. They were sentenced to life imprisonment.

6

Poison Pen

Today the village of Gedney lies just off the A17, which snakes its way across the southern edge of the Wash, roughly from Holbeach to Kings Lynn. Gedney is only a couple of miles from Holbeach. It's a village which appears in the Doomsday Book and in ancient times its church which stood on high ground was often surrounded by the sea at high tide. In fact as late as 1883 the Enclosure Bank, which had been built in 1874 to keep out the sea, collapsed and the whole area, called the marsh, was flooded to a depth of several feet. But by 1898 the Enclosure Bank had been rebuilt and the marsh was beginning to be drained and converted into rich farmland.

On a dark night in December of that year two men heard a woman weeping near a deep pit on the outskirts of the village. When they came nearer one of them, a Mr Bateman, recognised the woman. She was Eliza Bell, the wife of a local farm worker, and she was obviously in a distressed and highly excitable condition.

'Go away,' she shouted as Bateman came up to her, 'I'm going to do away with myself!'

But Bateman took her by the arm. 'Now now, lass. Let's have less of that! Whatever is the matter?'

'Let me go! Let me go!'

But eventually she calmed down somewhat and Bateman and the other man escorted her home as he knew where she lived. As they came up to the front garden gate of the farm worker's cottage, her husband Edward Bell came out of the front door.

'That's the trouble,' Eliza said to the two men, pointing at her husband coming up the garden path, 'and that trollop of his Mary Hodson.' Both men looked embarrassed, but Eliza carried on as if her husband wasn't there, although by this time he was standing by the gate and could hear every word she said. 'Do you know I've borne him five children? Three died, but I still have two at home. And I've been a good wife and made do on his very small wage. And what does he do? Carries on with a younger woman. Makes me the laughing stock of the village. And what does he say when I tackled him about it? Tells me she's better than me! I'm fed up. Fed up with him and fed up with my life.'

During all this Edward Bell, who was known as Ted, said nothing but he looked very uncomfortable. And the two men who had brought her home also looked discomforted. Eventually Bateman cleared his throat. 'I think we had better be off.'

Edward Bell, who had stood quietly by while all this was going on, said meekly, 'Will you come inside, Eliza?' And he opened the garden gate. She strode past without looking at him and went into the house.

Contemporary view of Gedney Church.

Eliza Bell was thirty and her husband was twenty-six. They had been living in the farm worker's cottage at Gedney for about five years. Next door lived the Hodsons, John and his wife. Their daughter Mary was twenty-two and she lived with her parents and her brothers and sisters. Everybody knew of the association between Mary and Edward and it wasn't only Eliza who disapproved. John Hodson was strongly against it and made his feelings known to Edward. The upshot was that the Bell family went away from Gedney and on 6 April 1899 they moved into a cottage at Weston, which is five miles from Spalding. Edward went to work for local farmer Mr Clayton as a farm yardman and labourer. He wrote to Mary soon after they moved in, but Mary subsequently burnt the letter and refused to tell anyone of its contents. But bad feeling continued between Eliza and Edward and quarrels were frequent.

The 22 June was a Saturday and Edward had the day off. He cycled into Spalding and called at the local branch of the Talbot Herbal Remedies Company, who were chemists and druggists and saw the manager Algernon Moulson.

'I'd like to buy some laudanum,' he said. 'I've heard it's very good for cuts and bruises and also toothache.'

Moulson scratched his head. 'I don't know about cuts and bruises, but it is certainly good for relieving toothache. Would a 2oz bottle be enough?'

Bell said that he thought it would. 'By the way, I'd also like to buy some white mercury.'

'Mercury?' said Moulson in surprise. 'That's a poison. What did you want it for?'

Bell hesitated a moment. 'I want to poison some rats in my house and back garden.'

'Well, you'll have to sign the poisons register, with your name and address and also give the name of someone who knows you here in the town.'

Edward thought for a moment. Then he gave his name, but his address he said was Holbeach Hurn, a small remote village out on the marsh. And when asked for someone who knew him, all he could think of was his employer Mr Clayton, who came into Spalding on market days. This seemed to satisfy Moulson and he then gave Bell two separate packets of mercury (II) chloride, more usually known at the time as 'corrosive sublimate'. The chemist duly noted the details in his book but when he came to the witness section – every sale was supposed to be witnessed and signed for by a person who knew the buyer – he merely put down 'Holbeach'.

Nearly all compounds of mercury are poisonous if taken in sufficient quantity, and even the vapour of the element, which at room temperature is a liquid, is highly toxic. But small amounts of mercury compounds have been used medicinally for many years as a laxative, an antiseptic and a treatment for syphilis. Large doses, however, particularly of corrosive sublimate, result in excessive salivation, stomach pains, violent vomiting and diarrhoea, insomnia, tremors, irritability and depression, and eventual death, but the patient can take a week or more to expire.

It was not very surprising then when the next day Eliza was taken ill with stomach pains. They were so severe that she called to her next door neighbour Mrs Buttress, who helped get her to bed and gave her some brandy. Edward came home at about seven or eight o'clock that night and he called the doctor. Dr Barritt of Spalding examined the patient and he believed that she was suffering from gastric irritation and he prescribed some medicine which contained an opiate and other soothing substances. Edward fetched a bottle and gave his wife a dose. But it did no good. In fact Eliza complained that the medicine burnt her as it went down her throat.

The next day, Monday, Eliza was very much worse. She now was in constant pain and her gums were bleeding. This is a common symptom of mercury poisoning. Edward told Mrs Buttress that she was not to have any more of the medicine. He would go into Spalding, see the doctor

Contemporary view of Weston village.

and get something more effective. He did so and got a new bottle of medicine, but he also paid another visit to Mr Moulson and asked for some more mercury. When Moulson asked him why he wanted it so quickly he explained that he had killed eight rats with it already but there were still more about his house. The chemist duly supplied Bell with some more corrosive sublimate.

Eliza had a very bad night and at four o'clock in the morning Edward rushed round to Mrs Buttress next door and asked her to come and help with his wife and his children. Mrs Buttress came round and after seeing Eliza, insisted that he call in the doctor again. Doctor Barritt arrived later that morning. Mrs Buttress asked him what he thought was the matter with Mrs Bell and he said that he thought that the initial irritation had progressed to inflammation of the bowels. He also said that the pain might be due to her passing a gall stone. Mrs Buttress told Edward that she thought he ought to call in Eliza's mother who lived near Skegness. Edward reported to his employer Mr Clayton that Eliza was very ill and asked him if he would send a telegram for him to Eliza's mother asking her to come as quickly as she could and that he would meet the evening train.

Mr Clayton sent the telegram and Edward Bell met the train later that evening and escorted a shocked and distressed Mrs Fox back to the cottage in Weston. On the way, Mrs Fox asked her son-in-law what the doctor had said he thought was the matter with her and Bell told her that the doctor had said that he thought she was suffering from gall stones. She also asked when the illness had begun and Bell said, 'I brought home some rolled bacon on Saturday night and by Sunday Eliza had begun to be sick.'

'What on earth possessed you to bring rolled bacon into the home when you already had bacon in the house?'

'Oh we just fancied it.'

Mrs Fox was appalled when she found the state her daughter was in, but Eliza continued to deteriorate during the night and when the early morning came Mrs Fox insisted that Bell go down to Spalding again and fetch the doctor. Dr Barritt arrived between six o'clock and seven o'clock that morning and gave Eliza an injection of morphine to ease her pain. Then he told Edward to go to Spalding and collect some more medicine. The farm worker went off at about seven o'clock that morning, but didn't return until twelve o'clock.

In the meantime he had called at the doctor's surgery and collected the new medicine. Then he went to the Talbot Herbal Remedies shop and saw Mr Moulson again.

'I've just run over one of my dogs,' said Bell. 'Can you give me something to kill it quickly, like arsenic?'

It was suggested at the trial that the arrival of Mrs Fox had precipitated a crisis for Bell. He no longer would be able to administer surreptitious doses of mercury and so he wanted to finish her off quickly.

Moulson looked doubtful. 'I can't give you any arsenic. Why don't you bring the dog here and I'll put it out of its misery for you.'

'I can't do that. It's much too ill to move. What about prussic acid? I've heard that's a very quick poison.'

'Good Heavens, I can't supply that. I tell you what though; lots of gamekeepers use strychnine to kill vermin, like foxes. I could let you have some of that.'

And so Edward Bell came away with six penny's worth of strychnine crystals ground down to a fine powder. He also called at Bell & White in Spalding and purchased some soda-water. When he got home Mrs Fox was waiting for him.

'You've been a very long time. We've been waiting for that new medicine to come.'

'I'm sorry about that. But the doctor had an important case to attend to and I had to wait a long time to see him. But he did give me a powder which he said would help to relieve her pain.'

Greetwell Prison today.

'He said nothing about a powder when he was here this morning.'

'Well, he must have had second thoughts, for he gave me some when I saw him. I'll just go up and give her it now.'

And with that he went upstairs. Mrs Fox had seen no powder, but she noticed that the new bottle of medicine which Bell had brought from the doctor that morning remained on the kitchen table. He had not taken it up to her daughter. She heard them talking upstairs in the bedroom and shortly afterwards Bell came downstairs. 'She's had some of the powder and I gave her half a glass of soda-water.' Then he sat down to dinner with Mrs Fox. During the meal he said, 'Everything that could be done for your daughter, you know, has been done.'

But as if to give the lie to his words, soon after that they heard terrible screams coming from above. They rushed upstairs to see Eliza writhing in agony on the bed. When she saw them she called out. 'Oh Ted. It must be that powder!'

'Nonsense. The doctor said it would settle you down.'

But they could not settle her down. They gave her brandy and applied warm towels to her feet, but it was all to no avail. Eliza Bell died within a few minutes. Later that evening Edward Bell made another trip to Spalding. He went to the doctor's surgery and told him that his wife had passed away peacefully about an hour after he got back home. The doctor, not having heard the real circumstances of her death, gave Bell a death certificate in accordance with his earlier diagnosis of inflammation of the bowels.

At that stage it seems that nobody was suspicious of the death and the funeral went ahead on Saturday 29 April. On the way to the funeral Bell stopped off at the post office and sent a telegram to Mary Hodson, who was on holiday at Barton-le-Clay, which is near Luton, and

THE LOUTH AND NORTH LINCOLNSHIRE NEWS—SATURDAY, JULY 8, 1899.

Answer to correspondent:—It was a mistake. The figures got transposed from 25 millions to 52 millions, somehow or other. In the year 1841 the population dependent on home-grown wheat was nearly 25 millions, to-day not half of that number can be so supplied, whilst more wheat is imported.

THE COUNTY SHOW AT LOUTH.

The preparations for the County Show at Louth have proceeded apace during the past week, and there is little doubt that everything will be in readiness for opening on Wednesday next. The street decorations, so far as present appearances go, will be on a magnificent scale. The route from the railway station to the show ground is admirably adapted for decorative purposes; and fine weather only is needed to crown the efforts of the Lincolnshire Agricultural Society and of our townspeople and the inhabitants of the district with the success which is so well deserved. The public luncheon will take place on Thursday at one o'clock on the show ground. Lord Heneage, the President for the year, will preside, and will be supported by Mr. R. W. Perks, M.P., the Mayor of Louth (Mr. Ald. Taylor), the [illegible] Steward (Mr. W. H. Smyth), Mr. T. [illegible]eney Garfit, and other gentlemen. The following is a programme of the arrangements:—

WEDNESDAY, JULY 12TH.

9.0 a.m.—Exhibition Opens. Public admitted on payment of 2/- each.
9.0 a.m.—Judging of Cattle (Ring No. 3), and of Sheep (Ring No. 4) and Pigs, to continue until completed.
9.0 a.m.—Judging of Hunters (Ring 1)—opposite the Grand Stand.

THE WIFE MURDER NEAR SPALDING.

THE CASE AT THE ASSIZES.

The Lincolnshire Summer Assizes were opened at the Castle, at Lincoln, on Monday, before Mr. Justice Lawrance. The principal case on the calendar was that in which Edward Bell (26), farm servant, of Weston Marsh, and formerly of Gedney, was charged with the wilful murder of his wife, Eliza Bell (30), by poisoning her with strychnine and mercury at Weston Marsh, Spalding, on the 26th of April. The allegation is, it will be remembered, that the accused administered the mercury to his wife in medicine while she was under the medical care of Dr. Barritt, of Spalding, and that he gave her the strychnine in a powder, under the pretence that it had been sent by the doctor to soothe her.

Mr. Justice Lawrance arrived in Lincoln on Saturday, but business was not commenced until Monday, when, after opening the City Court, his lordship arrived at the Castle at 11 a.m.

THE JUDGE'S CHARGE.

His Lordship, in addressing the Grand Jury, referred to the murder charge, and said that he did not intend to trouble them with any observations, beyond a slight sketch of the case, in order that they might see what part of it was material for their attention to be directed. It seemed that the prisoner, Edward Bell, who had been married to his wife a few years, was in the employ of Mr. Clayton, and living in some Marsh near Spalding. About the 24th of April, Mr. Clayton became aware that the wife was unwell, and the husband went on two or three occasions to Spalding about five miles distant—to fetch a doctor to his wife. The doctor attended her from that time to the day of her death, which was on the 26th of April, and the prisoner went to Spalding each day, for the purpose of bringing medicine from the doctor. Now, during the time of his visit to Spalding, he also went to a place called the Talbot Herbal Remedies Company's Limited, carrying on business as chemists and druggists, at Spalding. He came on the first occasion, according to the evidence of the manager, upon the 22nd of April, and he made some excuse, but he need not trouble the Grand Jury at any length with it. He asked for some laudanum, saying he wanted it for the toothache, or something of that kind. He then asked for some white mercury, which he said he wanted to poison some rats with. The manager asked him his name and where he lived. He said his name was Bell, and he lived at Holbeach Hurn—true as far as his name was concerned, and false as far as the address. Asked if there was anyone in the town who knew him, he replied in the negative, and said that his employer, Mr. Clayton, came up on market days. Without any further ado, and without enquiring any further, the chemist supplied the prisoner with an ounce of perchloride of mercury, duly labelled. He entered the sale in his book, as he was bound to do under the Statue, but when he came to the place of the signature of the person introducing the purchaser—because every person supplied with poison should be witnessed by someone—the only entry was

Mrs. Buttress, who lived in the cottage next door to that occupied by Bell and his wife. She was apparently suffering from irritation of the stomach, and she continued ill from Sunday, April 23rd, until about one o'clock on Wednesday, April 26th, when she died. During those three days she was seen by Mrs. Buttress from time to time. She was seen by Dr. Barritt, of Spalding, who was called in on three or four occasions, and on Tuesday night before her death her mother, Mrs. Fox, came to Arby, where she was then living, and attended her from that night till the time she died on Wednesday, April 26th. She was buried on the 29th. On the 8th of May a letter was received by Mrs. Fox, and that letter Mrs. Fox forwarded to the police at Spalding. The result was that inquiries were made, and the body of Mrs. Bell was exhumed some days afterwards. In consequence of the Coroner's warrant a post-mortem examination was held by Dr. Walker, of Spilsby, and Dr. Thompson, of Burgh, and the result would be given in evidence. Parts of the body were sent up to Dr. Stephenson, the analyst, in London, and he made an analysis. When they heard the evidence and the symptoms which attended the illness of the poor woman between April 23rd and 26th, and when they heard the medical evidence, they would not have the shadow of a doubt in their minds, if they believed that evidence, that two sorts of poison had been administered to the woman shortly before her death, one of these poisons being perchloride of mercury, a mineral irritant poison, and the other, the vegetable poison strychnine. Quantities of both these poisons were found in her body, and counsel invited the jury to believe on the evidence he would call that the poisons were wickedly and wilfully administered to the deceased by the prisoner at the bar. Alluding to the married life of the prisoner and his deceased wife, he said that at any rate during the last year and the beginning of this year their married life was undoubtedly, an unhappy one. While living at Gedney the prisoner seemed to have formed the acquaintance of a girl named Hodson, who lived in a cottage next door to the cottage in which he and his wife lived. He would call that girl before them, and he would prove that there were quarrels between the prisoner and his wife, and he would mention one circumstance which, he said, would show the unhappy state of things which was going on between the prisoner and his wife. In December last year, about 8 o'clock in the evening, the prisoner's wife, Mary Eliza Bell, was found crying bitterly near a pit in the neighbourhood of Gedney, and she was so found by two gentlemen—a Mr. Chapman and Mr. Bateman. Mr. Bateman took her home, and prisoner met them at the gate, and a conversation took place about the girl Hodson, and the wife told Mr. Chapman in the prisoner's presence, and he did not deny it, that she was tired of her life, and that the trouble was owing to this girl Hodson. She said further that Bell had told her that the girl Hodson was better than she. That was the state of things when they came to Weston, and there was unhappiness and irritation about the girl, and recrimination and quarrels took place between the prisoner and his wife. Coming to Saturday, April 22nd, the day before Mrs. Bell became ill, the prisoner went to Spalding, five miles away, and

Fox remarked that he had been a long time, and the prisoner said that the doctor had an important case to attend to and caused him to wait. That was not true, and nothing of the sort had occurred at the time. Then the accused said to Mrs. Fox. "The doctor has given me a powder," and that was absolutely false, as the doctor had given him no such thing. The only thing that Dr. Barritt had given him at that time was a bottle of medicine, which he brought home and put on the table in Mrs. Fox's presence. The only thing in the nature of a powder which he could have about him was the strychnine which he had brought from Moulson, at Spalding, that morning. Mrs. Fox said, "The doctor said nothing about the powder," but the prisoner replied, "He gave me one." Mrs. Fox, however, never saw the powder, for prisoner said, "I will go up and give it to her." Prisoner was in his wife's bedroom about five minutes, and Mrs. Fox heard him talking to her daughter, and then the accused came down again and remarked, "She has taken 'it' and half a glass of soda too." "It" meant the powder, the bottle was downstairs, and had never gone up. The poor woman never had it. Then the prisoner sat down to dinner with Mrs. Fox, and they began to talk. The prisoner said, "Everything that could be done has been done for her," but in a very short time screams were heard from the bedroom, and they both ran upstairs and found the poor woman in a terrible condition, apparently suffering the most frightful agony. They did what they could, gave her brandy and applied hot water to her feet, but in a few minutes the wife died with all the usual symptoms and with all the terrible agony which accompanied that most frightful of deaths—death by poisoning from strychnine. That same evening the prisoner went to Spalding again, and went to Dr. Barritt, and asked for a certificate of death, and prisoner's account of what had taken place was "she passed away quietly about an hour after I had got home." The funeral took place on the 29th of April, and on the way to lay his wife in the grave he sent a telegram to the girl Hodson, asking her to meet him, and on the Monday he went to see her, and became engaged to be married to her two days after he had laid his wife in the grave. Two days afterwards Mrs. Fox received a letter, which she sent to the police at Spalding, and on the 9th of May Superintendent Osborne and Inspector Peach went and saw the prisoner at his own house. Counsel then proceeded to dealt with the discovery of bottles on the prisoner's premises, and with the steps taken to have the body exhumed.

THE EVIDENCE.

Mr. Thomas Clayton, farmer, Spalding Marsh, said that the prisoner had been his farm yardman. He came to him on April 6th last. He came to him from Mr. Snushall's, of Gedney.—Cross-examined by Mr. Bousey: Witness stated that the prisoner said he would like his wife's mother to see her, and he (witness) sent a telegram from Spalding to his wife's mother to come at prisoner's request. Prisoner appeared anxious to do all he could for his wife.

Mrs. Buttress, wife of a horsekeeper for Mr. Clayton, described the sufferings of Mrs. Bell at the time of her death, and said that Mrs. Bell said "Oh, Ted, it must be that powder."

Headline from the *Louth and North Lincolnshire News* for Saturday 8 July 1899.

arranged to meet her. He had already written to her soon after his wife's death telling her what had happened. On the following Monday, he travelled to Barton-le-Clay and met Mary Hodson. He asked her to marry him and she agreed and they became formally engaged. It seems that Mary was full of plans for the wedding and afterwards, for she wrote to Edward saying that she thought they should have at least one of his children to live with them after they were married.

It is possible that Bell would have got away with the murder, although in small villages rumours soon arise and might in time have reached the ears of the police or Dr Barritt. But all this is speculation, since Bell himself had an attack of conscience. Perhaps he felt sorry for his wife's mother in her obvious distress at her daughter's death, or possibly he felt guilty over his precipitous association with Mary Hodson. At all events Mrs Fox received a letter two days after his meeting with Mary. It said, 'I cannot keep it any longer. The doctor never sent that powder. I am miserable about it. See the doctor about it. He will tell you the same. I am going away tomorrow. I cannot stop here.'

Mrs Fox passed the letter over to the Spalding Police and on 9 May Superintendent Osborne visited Dr Barritt. Then he went on to Bell & White in Spalding, the Talbot Herbal Remedies shop and finally to Mr Clayton's farm where he saw Edward Bell. When questioned, Bell said that the powder he had given his wife was magnesia, which he had bought at Bell & White. But the staff at that shop denied having sold him any. Mr Moulson also picked Bell out of an identification parade as the man to whom he had sold mercury and strychnine and after that Bell was charged with the willful murder of his wife. The superintendent searched in and around the premises at Weston and found several medicine bottles prescribed by Dr Barritt. One, which had

The assize court at Lincoln Castle.

been concealed under a hedge, proved to contain traces of mercury, which suggested that Bell had doctored his wife's medicine with corrosive sublimate. The body of Eliza Bell was exhumed and a post mortem carried out. The organs showed the unmistakable presence of mercury and strychnine.

The trial at the Summer Assizes, held in the castle at Lincoln, opened on Tuesday 4 July before Mr Justice Lawrance. The prosecution was in the hands of Mr Appleton and Mr Bonner and the defence was conducted by Mr H.D. Bonsey. Evidence was given by the police, Mrs Fox, Mrs Buttress, Mr Moulson and others. The defence counsel had a difficult job and contented himself with asking the jury not to be swayed by the prisoner's immorality. But the verdict was a foregone conclusion and the jury took only a few minutes to arrive at a guilty verdict. The judge donned the black cap and pronounced the sentence of death. This was carried out on 25 July at the Greetwell Road Prison in Lincoln. James Billington had been booked to perform the execution, but his son William turned up instead, saying that his father was ill and had sent him in his place. William Billington was not on the approved list of executioners, but the Prison Governor rather than delay the proceedings decided to go ahead with the son and William performed the hanging.

7

Someone has Killed our Joan

It was a dark December night in 1948 as Herbert Mason, who was forty, pushed his cycle up the side of his house in Queensway, Scunthorpe and into the back yard. It was a Wednesday and he had just come off the 7 a.m. to 5 p.m. shift at the Appleby-Frodingham Steelworks. He locked the cycle away in the shed and turned to walk back towards the house. It was then that he noticed that the lights were not on. This was odd as his housekeeper Mrs Green at least should have been home. His wife had died in 1944 and Mason had not married again. He had had a series of housekeepers to live in and look after him and his fourteen year old daughter Joan. Mrs Hilda Green, who was forty-one, had been with him since November 20 when she had answered an advertisement he had put in the local paper a little under a month before.

As he walked towards the back door however, some lights were switched on in the house. He opened the back door, went into the scullery and switched on the light. As he washed himself in the sink he noticed that the floor was wet. But as it was wash day he thought no more about it. He found Mrs Green in the sitting room and asked her about the lights, but she said she had been upstairs making the beds. She got him his evening meal and afterwards he sat down with the paper.

'Joan gone to the pictures, then, has she?' he asked.

Mrs Green said that Joan had not been home for her midday meal and showed him some food she had cooked for her. Mr Mason was not unduly worried as Joan sometimes went to the pictures in the afternoon with her friends. But after some time he began to feel uneasy. Mrs Green said she thought Joan might be out with a boy. 'If she has been enticed away by some lad they will have a struggle with Joan for she is very strong,' she laughed.

But Mason didn't think that she had any boyfriends and after a time he decided to go round to one of his daughter's friends and see if she was there. Silvia Drinkall, who lived nearby in North Parade, Ashby, said that she had not seen her friend since they had left school to go home for lunch. But when she called at the house in Queensway at just before five that afternoon Mrs Green told her that Joan had not been home to lunch. Another friend, Marina Stratford, said that she left Joan at just after midday and they had arranged to meet at 1.15 p.m. but she never turned up.

A very puzzled and worried Herbert Mason returned home that night. As he walked up the yard he saw a dark shape on the ground outside the back door. He quickly opened the back door and switched on the scullery light. Then he saw that it was the body of his daughter. She was lying on her face with her legs stretched out behind her and her skirt was pulled up around her waist. He could see blood on her head and when he felt her skin, it was cold.

'Come here Mrs Green,' he cried in a broken voice. 'Someone has killed our Joan!'

The police were called and the local police doctor, Dr Robert Eminson officially pronounced the girl dead. He also said that he thought the child had been dragged along the ground on her face. Later at the post mortem, conducted by Dr David Hamilton Fulton at the Peterborough Memorial Hospital, extensive fractures of the skull were discovered. When at the magistrates' court he was shown a metal bar about eighteen inches long with a flattened end which was bent over at right angles (in fact a fire iron rake), he agreed that it could have caused the injuries. The pathologist also examined the contents of the stomach and gave it as his opinion that death must have occurred within forty-five minutes of a meal having being eaten. Although the body, when discovered, had the appearance of a sex attack – the skirt was drawn up and the underclothes disturbed and torn – he said that there was no medical evidence of a sexual assault.

When Inspector Leslie Kirby arrived at the house in Queensway he questioned Herbert Mason and Mrs Green. Mason said that as far as he knew his daughter had no boyfriends, only the girlfriends she had at school, which was the Ashby Girls' Secondary School.

'Has she been writing to anybody recently, or received any letters lately?'

'As far as I know she hasn't.'

But Mrs Green chimed in, 'She used to get letters from a soldier. I only know his first name, which was Charlie. I don't know anything about him except that Joan said that he was coming to see her at Christmas.'

'And did she receive letters from him?' asked the inspector.

'Yes, I believe so.'

Queensway where the Masons and Mrs Green lived (Courtesy of the North Lincolnshire Museums Service Image archives).

'Could I see the letters?'

'No, Joan sent them all back.'

'You don't know where they came from?'

'No, I don't.'

But the inspector was not satisfied and he and his men made a search of the house. In the living room he noticed that there was a large dark stain on the carpet. It was damp in places as if somebody had tried to wash it out. And when the carpet was taken up blood was discovered underneath it. There were also stains which looked very much like blood on top of the wash copper in the scullery. In the dustbin outside the back door was found a sack, with again what looked very much like blood stains on it. And in a cupboard he found the fire rake, but it was surprisingly clean.

Detective Sergeant Clarricoates made a search of Joan's room. He found no letters, but Mrs Green who had accompanied him said that Joan was in the habit of coming home late when her father was on nights.

'She often came in as late as 11.45 p.m. Once she said she had been out with some boys and had missed the last bus home.'

But Herbert Mason, when he was interviewed, told a different story. He said that from the very first Joan and Mrs Green had not got on with each other and there were frequent quarrels. About a week before the murder Joan noticed that one of her coats had a large tear in the back. She told her father, who later questioned Mrs Green, but she denied having anything to do with it. Then a few nights later Joan returned from the pictures at about ten o'clock. It had been agreed beforehand that both she and Mrs Green, who was also out, would arrive back at

North Parade, Ashby, the home of one of Joan Mason's girlfriends.

10 p.m. But Joan had to wait an hour and a half in the air raid shelter in the back garden until Mrs Green came home. When Mason came home later Mrs Green told him that Joan had been in bed for hours. The next morning Joan complained to her father about Mrs Green. When he asked her about it she said that Joan was telling lies and that she had heard Joan with a boy in the air raid shelter. Mason didn't believe her and gave her notice.

On the Saturday before the murder, a woman went into the Scunthorpe Branch of the Lincoln Savings Bank and was seen by Mrs Joyce Pascoe who worked there part time. The woman produced a 'pay bearer' form and book signed by Joan Mason and signed on the back 'Mrs Mason'. Mrs Pascoe dully paid over the ten pounds asked for and the woman chatted for a while, saying she was hot as she had been rushing. She said the money was for the girl who was going away for Christmas. She was an only child and she had been very much spoiled. Herbert Mason said afterwards that the writing on the forms resembled Mrs Green's. And Mrs Pascoe picked out Mrs Green at an identification parade as the woman who had cashed the cheque.

Mrs Green was charged with murder. She was asked if she wanted to say anything and she asked Inspector Kirby if she could say yes or no. He told her she could say anything she wished and she replied, 'I don't want to say anything.' Later she made a statement about the blood on the carpet, saying that it came from a wart on Joan's leg which had bled profusely.

The murder was the sensation of Scunthorpe. At the funeral which took place on Tuesday 21 December, large crowds braved the bitterly cold weather and lined the paths at the Brumby Cemetery. Eight of Joan's school friends, each carrying a bunch of violets, acted as a guard-of-honour at the house and the cemetery. The pathway to the grave was lined with flowers mostly from friends and neighbours, workmates of Herbert Green and young people from St Paul's Church, Ashby, which Joan had attended.

Hilda Green was committed for trial at the Lincolnshire Assizes in February by the Scunthorpe Magistrates on Thursday 27 January. But an application was made by one of her counsel, Mr J.A. Grieves, to Mr Justice Lynsky at the Leicester Assizes for the trial to be transferred from the Lincolnshire to the Nottinghamshire Assizes to allow more time for medical observation of his client. This was granted and the trial began on Monday 28 February

Ashby High Street (Courtesy of the North Lincolnshire Museums Service Image Archives).

St Paul's Church, Ashby, today.

1949 at the small court room in Nottingham. The trial was the sensation of Scunthorpe and a bus load of witnesses, relatives and schoolgirl friends of Joan Mason left the town early that day for Nottingham. It was half an hour late starting because Hilda Green's mother, Mrs Ada Green, had gone to the wrong pick-up point.

The prosecution was led by Mr A. Ward and Mr W. Sime. Their case was that Joan had to cycle about a mile to go to school and used to go home for her lunch at twelve o'clock every day, rain or shine. On the day of the murder she was seen by school friends on her way home within 200 yards of the Queensway house. At 3.30 p.m that day a coal man left five hundredweights of coal at the house and saw a cycle by the garden fence which was identical to the one Joan had been riding. Later that day it was found by a policeman further down Queensway. Joan had been murdered shortly after she had had her meal. The body was then left in the sitting room until it was dark, which would account for the blood on the carpet there. Then it was moved when Mr Mason came home and when he went looking for her, it was dragged to the outside door where it was subsequently found. Examination of the bloodstains showed that the sack found in the dustbin, the sitting room carpet, the settee cover and a cushion from the settee, and an apron, all had human blood group 'O' on them, which was Joan's blood group, whereas Mrs Green's blood group was 'A'.

When Mr R. Vaughan opened the defence it was plain that he was going for an insanity plea. He didn't challenge any of the prosecution's case and complained that Mrs Green had not been helpful or cooperative in her defence. She did not go into the witness box. Mr Vaughan brought witnesses to show her instability. Her sister Mrs Kathleen Wray spoke of their unhappy childhood with a physically abusive father. Once when she was twenty, after a row with her father, she threw herself into the River Ancholme and Mrs Wray herself helped to rescue her. On another occasion her father was involved in a fight with some men. One of them tried to hit their father with a spade and instead hit Hilda on the head instead. Her head was badly cut

Brumby Cemetery (Courtesy of the North Lincolnshire Museums Service Image Archives).

and a doctor had to be fetched. After the death of her first husband she began to have delusions and imagined that she could see her husband. In 1939 she married again, but the short marriage was ended when her second husband was killed at Dunkirk.

Mr George Duckett, a farmer, said that he employed Hilda when she was about twenty and found her very peculiar. Once after an altercation with one of the farm hands she was found lying on the grass in her night dress, but could remember nothing of it the next day. Hilda Green's daughter, Mrs Kathleen Walker who was nineteen, said her mother often complained of headaches and on occasion she lost her memory as well. She had threatened her daughter with a poker, but had never hit her with one. She was reminded of an incident when she and her mother were lodging with an old man who was one day found with a head wound. Her mother admitted to her that she had hit him with a poker, which was afterwards found in their room. But nothing came of the incident. Also brought in was evidence that Mrs Green had worked for some doctors in Bridlington but she was eventually discharged because they considered her mentally unstable. On the other hand doctors brought in by the prosecution who had observed her at Strangeways Prison were of the opinion that she was not insane and though she might be dull-witted, she would know what she was doing was right or wrong (one of the legal tests for insanity at the time).

The jury which contained three women took only twenty-five minutes to bring in a verdict of guilty. The clerk of the assizes asked her if she had anything to say before sentence was passed and she answered, 'No, sir' in an almost inaudible voice. The judge put on the black cap and intoned the death sentence. Her appeal was heard on 24 March and dismissed by the Lord Chief Justice, Lord Goddard. Her execution was fixed for Saturday 9 April, but on the Wednesday before the Home Secretary, Mr Chuter Ede, granted a reprieve and Mrs Green was sentenced to life imprisonment.

8

Murder in the North Sea

Before 1889 the northern part of Grimsby around the dock area stretched only as far as Victor Street. The area to the East and going as far as Park Street was part of the Clee-with-Weelsby parish known as New Clee. But in 1889 it was added to the borough of Grimsby, bringing the population to just over 50,000, and making it eligible for county borough status, which it obtained in 1891. It was an area of low cost housing occupied mostly by families associated with fishing and the docks. This was the boom era of fishing in Grimsby. In 1906 the population had risen to 76,000 and over 500 fishing vessels were registered in the port. They were mostly fishing smacks, sail driven vessels with a crew usually of five. They used the trawl method of fishing and usually fished in the North Sea.

At 160 Kent Street lived William Connelly, who was forty-two and married with two children, one four years old and the other three months. He had held a skipper's certificate for several years and was one of the top skippers of the Grimsby Ice Company which had been founded in 1861 and owned eighty-five sailing smacks. On Friday 22 February 1889 he set sail in the Grimsby Ice Company's trawl smack *Doncaster* for a fishing trip in the North Sea. It was the first time that he had sailed in the vessel and it was to be his last. Three weeks later, on Thursday 14 March in the early hours of the morning, the vessel arrived back in port. But she carried more than fish in the hold. She carried the dead body of Skipper Connelly. And also in confinement was the cook, Walter Gempton, an eighteen year old apprentice. When the vessel docked Arthur Turrell, the second hand, who lived at 23 Duke Street in New Clee, and who was in charge of the vessel in the absence of the skipper, handed over the young boy to Dock Constable Lawton, to be charged with murder.

The body of the unfortunate skipper was taken to the mortuary at the hospital to await the coroner's inquest and a post mortem was performed. Young Gempton was first lodged in the Borough Branch Lock-up and then transferred to the cells at the Town Hall. Normally he lodged with his parents in Grafton Street and was the eldest of six children. His mother was the sister of Skipper Connelly's wife. Since puberty he had suffered from a condition which was probably epilepsy. He had frequent fits of the *grand mal* variety. They usually only lasted for a few minutes but he was often disorientated for a time afterwards. And the fits were often so violent that he frequently injured himself. About eighteen months before the fatal trip he was an out-patient at Grimsby Hospital, having badly scalded himself during a fit by falling into a large pan, described at the time as a pancheon, full of boiling water. Since at the time there were none of the drugs available today to alleviate the condition of epilepsy it is a wonder that he was able to obtain any employment at all. But the call for apprentice boys to help man the smacks was

Kent Street (Courtesy of the *Grimsby Telegraph* Archives).

very strong at the time. Quite often the major portion of the crew would be apprentices. And Walter Gempton was able to find a berth. It is true he usually sailed with his father who was also a skipper, but this time he sailed as a cook with his uncle.

The inquest opened at the hospital on the afternoon of Friday 15 March by the coroner Alderman Moody. J.P. Superintendent Waldram brought the young lad to the court. Gempton was seen to be considerably scarred over the right eye and the left arm owing to falls he had had during fits he suffered while in custody. He seemed to take little notice of the proceedings, playing with his cap, or examining his scars or sitting with folded arms. Occasionally he shook his head and whispered to himself. But when he was spoken to his answers were clear and prompt.

The first witness called was Arthur Turrell, the second hand on the *Doncaster*. He described sailing from Grimsby on the 22 February. On the 11 March they were about 240 miles East North East of Spurn. About six o'clock in the evening they were just about to begin fishing and were ready to launch the net. He was on deck with the skipper. They were standing talking near the companionway which led down below decks. There was another deck-hand on the deck and the cook, Walter Gempton, was on the port side. He appeared to be walking up and down with his hands in his pockets, muttering to himself. Suddenly he rushed at the skipper and struck him at the back of the neck.

'I didn't see the knife at first. The skipper fell to the deck shouting, "He's stabbed me!" The cook fell on top of him. I grabbed Gempton and pulled him off the skipper. Then the skipper got up and rushed down below and I followed. He fell upon his locker and then I saw blood gushing out of his neck. The skipper said, "Put some flour on it to stop the bleeding." I rushed

Grimsby Hospital (Courtesy of the Grimsby Telegraph Archives).

through to the galley and got some flour in a large jar. Then came back and shook it on the skipper's neck. But I couldn't stop the bleeding. The skipper cried, "Stop the blood, Jim, if you can and I might live." But I couldn't.'

'And how long did he live from the time of the stab?' asked the coroner.

'About ten minutes.'

The coroner then asked, 'Was there much loss of blood externally?'

'Yes, sir. He lost a large quantity of blood.' The coroner then asked if there was anything that the skipper had done to provoke the prisoner to do this terrible thing.

'No sir.'

'To your knowledge there had been no quarrel? No difference of opinion between the deceased and the prisoner?'

'No sir.'

'Did you hear the prisoner say anything at all to him?'

'Yes sir. When I pulled him off the skipper. He said the skipper was Jack the Ripper and he wanted to make off with the ship and all hands.'

It will be remembered that the celebrated Jack the Ripper case occurred only the year before, in 1888. An unknown murderer stalked the streets of Whitechapel, in London's East End, and killed five prostitutes within a three month period. His victims had their throats cut and most were savagely mutilated. The case inspired a comment from Queen Victoria, caused a furore in the government and frustrated the Metropolitan Police Commissioner to the point of resignation. The whole country was agog with the doings of the murderer and the letters apparently sent by

Grimsby Town Hall (Courtesy of the North East Lincolnshire Library Archives).

him to the newspapers. So it was no surprise that Gempton should accuse the skipper of being Jack the Ripper. Many men had also been accused of being the fiendish murderer.

'And did the prisoner say anything else?'

'That was while he was still on deck. He called down through the skylight while the skipper was lying on his bunk. 'You crafty old b------, that's settled you! That's a bit of Jack the Ripper!'

Turrell also said that when the skipper had died he asked Gempton to come down and see his uncle. The young lad did so and when he bent over the body Turrell grasped him from behind and tied him up. Then he put him in a cabin and set sail for Grimsby.

He was also questioned by members of the jury. A coroner's court had much less strict rules of evidence than a magistrates' court or a trial at an assize court. And in this case there was considerable comment from the jury about the case in questions they put to witnesses. Turrell was asked by jury members if Gempton had seemed to be sorry for what he had done.

'Sometimes,' replied Turrell, 'he talked as if he did. And sometimes he talked is if he didn't. And he did not say why he had done it.'

Another juror commented that he had heard that the skipper had ill-treated another lad on board his vessel and knocked his teeth out. Turrell could not confirm this. Another said that he had been informed that the skipper had savagely assaulted his wife. Mr Broadhead, the solicitor who appeared for Gempton, admitted that this was true. The deceased had been summoned before the magistrates two or three times for assaulting his wife, once in the early part of this year. He was a man who drank a great deal.

Grafton Street (Courtesy of the *Grimsby Telegraph* Archives).

Henry Crew who was a deck hand residing at 55 Trinity Street was the next witness. He confirmed Turrell's account and again said that he had heard no quarrelling between the skipper and Gempton. He said that he had only seen Gempton have two fits since he came on board but he believed that he had others, but they had occurred while he had been below. After the attack he had gone up on deck and lit a red flare. By its light he and the rest of the crew made a search for the knife. He found it lying on the deck by the port side. It was an ordinary clasp knife.

The coroner asked, 'Did you see any blood on the knife?'

'Well I saw something and I took it to be blood.' A juror asked if he had ever seen the prisoner with the knife.

'Yes,' replied Crew. 'I know it is his knife, for I have seen him using it in cleaning fish and the like.'

Walter Gempton was asked if he had any questions for this witness or the last and he said that he hadn't.

The medical evidence came next. Dr Stephenson said that he had done the post mortem on the deceased and was asked to describe what he found.

'I found a wound on the back of the neck on the left side, half an inch in length and four inches in depth, penetrating through the muscles to the vertebral column at its junction with the skull, passing between the joint and severing the left vertebral artery, causing bleeding and a clot of blood on the brain. The pressure of the clot would be the cause of death.'

'He bled both internally and externally?' asked the coroner.

'Yes.'

A trawl smack (Courtesy of Stuart Sizer).

A juror asked if the doctor thought that the effects of the fits that the prisoner suffered might be temporary insanity.

'It might be. The fits to which he was subject generally end in insanity.'

The coroner then asked if the wound would be likely to be caused by the knife produced in court. And the doctor answered that he thought it would. The coroner then addressed the prisoner.

'After hearing the evidence have you anything to say in answer to the charge against you?'

'I cannot say whether I was in my right senses or not, or in a fit.'

In his summing up the coroner said that it was not the duty of the jury to consider the question of insanity. They had to decide the cause of death. If they followed the medical evidence it suggested that he died from the effects of the wound.

'Your verdict,' he said, 'will of course be as to what was the cause of death. If you are satisfied that Gempton caused the wound and that the skipper died as a consequence. I cannot see what other verdict you can give, but one of wilful murder.' The jury brought in a verdict to that effect.

At the magistrates' court held the following Monday at the Borough Police Court, Mrs Gempton, the prisoner's mother, was present. She seemed very distressed as the evidence against

Trinity Street (Courtesy of the North East Lincolnshire Library Archives).

THE MURDER OF A GRIMSBY FISHERMAN AT SEA.

INQUEST AND VERDICT.

'WILFUL MURDER' AGAINST THE LAD GEMPTON.

On Friday afternoon last, the Coroner for the district, Mr. Alderman Moody, J.P., opened the inquest on the body of William Conolly, skipper of the smack Doncaster, who at sea, on Monday last, died from a wound inflicted with a knife by the cook of the vessel, Walter Tennant Gempton. The following gentlemen were sworn on the jury :—Messrs. Chas. Andrews (foreman), Jno. Kirk, Geo. Hewitt, R. C. Benton, R. A. Ray, C. Burnham, C. Summer, Geo. Warner, J. C. Smith, R. Beels, R. Graves, and J. Eastwood. Supt. Waldram brought the prisoner to the Hospital before the jury. The lad is considerably scarred over the right eye and left arm, owing to falls during the fits to which he is subject. He appeared little concerned with the proceedings or his position. He played with his cap at one time, and examined the hurts on his arm now and again, and at another time sat with folded arms—occasionally shaking his head and whispering to himself. When spoken to, however, his answers were prompt and intelligent. Dr. Stephenson (hon. surgeon) and Dr. Dorman (house surgeon) attended the inquiry. Inspector Foster, of the Dock-police, and P.c. Long, who had charge of the prisoner, were also present. After the jury had viewed the body, the following evidence was taken :—

Part of a newspaper report from the *Grimsby News*, 22 March 1889.

her son was presented and the town clerk asked her if she would prefer to leave the court but she said that she would stay and a chair was brought for her, as normally the general public were expected to stand.

The evidence of Arthur Turrell and Henry Crew was presented and after this the prisoner was asked if he had anything he wished to say in reply. He said, 'I cannot remember ever handling the knife. I must have been void of sense when I did it.'

Superintendent Waldram reported that he had been handed a letter by Mr Davis, the port missionary. It was a letter written by Skipper Connelly to his wife during the voyage and contained the passage:

Walter has had no less than four fits since we came out, three in one day, and the worst you never know when they are coming on... I have saved that bottle with hartshorn in (hartshorn was the old name for sal volatile or ammonium carbonate), for when Walter goes off and we clap it under his nose, and he gets two or three good sniffs, it soon brings him out of the fit; but he is a long time kind of silly after.

The town clerk asked the prisoner if he had anything to say and he replied, 'No; I don't know that I have anything to say gentlemen.'

Walter Gempton was then committed for trial at the assizes on a charge of wilful murder. But when the trial opened on Saturday 20 July 1889 at the Lincoln Assizes and the jury were empanelled and heard the indictment read, the dock where the prisoner normally stood was empty. The judge, Mr Justice Hawkins, addressed the jury. He told them that Walter Tennant Gempton was the prisoner and he outlined the case against him. Then he said that on a point of law a man who deliberately caused the death of another was guilty of wilful murder. It was no part of the jury's province to inquire into the state of the prisoner's mind at the time. All they had to consider was whether he had wilfully killed the man and in this case he did not think the jury would have any difficulty in the matter.

'Gempton is,' continued the judge, 'at the present moment in a lunatic asylum and perhaps would not be a position to take his trial.'

The jury duly brought in a verdict of guilty of murder and the trial was over. Nothing more was heard of Walter Gempton and it must be presumed that he spent the rest of his life in an asylum.

9

The Amorous Pork Butcher

Mary Ann Garner did not have a lot of luck with her men. She was thirty-two and lived at 19 Stanley Place, which in 1891 was a turning off Chelmsford Street, in Lincoln. She was the widow of Henry Garner who for some years was the ostler at the Queen Hotel in the city. But he became insane and was removed to the Lincolnshire County Lunatic Asylum, now known as The Lawns, where he died in August 1889. He had been ten years older than Mary, who was his second wife, and he left her with six children. Two of them – John and Annie – were the children from the first marriage. Then he had another four with Mary; Ethel, who was eight when this story begins, Arthur, who was six, Ernest, who was five and little Ada who was four. John was fifteen and an apprentice at the foundry of Robey & Co, and Annie, who was thirteen, was in domestic service in London. Ethel was also in London staying with an aunt. But this left four children at home, only one of whom was bringing in any wages. But Mary worked very hard, taking in washing and mending, going out cleaning and taking in lodgers.

She had lived with her brood not far away in Stanley Terrace, a turning off Ripon Street, for a couple of years previously, but about six weeks earlier in January 1891, they had moved to 19 Stanley Place. She took in lodgers mainly from the employees of Mr Nissler, a pork butcher in the High Street, with whom her brother had formerly been employed.

One of Mr Nissler's employees had been Arthur Spencer. At twenty-two he was ten years younger than Mrs Garner and had lodged with her for nearly a year. He was described as a tall but rather stout man. He originally came from Blyth in Nottinghamshire, where his parents were still living, his father being a carrier there. Arthur Spencer had been employed by Mr Nissler, but after about nine months he had been dismissed for reasons which remain obscure and had been unemployed since then. He continued to lodge with the widow however and she had not charged him rent since he had no money coming in.

About the beginning of March 1891 Spencer obtained employment with Mr West, a pork butcher whose shop was on Waterside. Mr West engaged him for a month, but one of the conditions of his employment was that he should live over the shop. He went to live there but left his box with his clothes and some of his belongings in it at Mrs Garner's house. He was said to be a frequent visitor to the Stanley Place house and indeed to have only stayed at Mr West's house for three or four nights a week, while the other nights he stayed at his old lodgings.

The relationship between Spencer and Mrs Garner seems to have been complex. Plainly he was infatuated with her since he was always asking her to marry him, but although she had initially been kind and cordial towards him, she now seemed to be resisting his advances. And

Contemporary view of Chelmsford Street at the corner with Cross Street.

when she knew that his present job with Mr West was coming to an end and she realised that he would want to come back and live off her again, she began to put him off.

'No,' she said when he had again asked her to marry him. And when he tried to induce her to let him come back and lodge with her she said, 'We are separated now and it will be better that we remain separated.'

On Friday 27 March he again came to see her and renewed his entreaties for her to marry him or at least to let him come back and live with her. But she said, 'I have to work hard to keep myself and my children and I cannot afford to keep you in idleness.'

This remark points to the realities of the situation. Obviously Spencer wanted to marry the widow, but he was also looking for a comfortable billet. He was looking for a woman who was hard working and would support him when he was out of work. But he finally became incensed at Mary's refusal to marry him and replied, 'Then if you won't have me, no other man will have you, for I will shoot you and then shoot myself too.' But his words cut no ice with Mrs Garner and he left soon after, muttering to himself.

At about 9.30 p.m the following evening George Porter was in the shop of Mr Hanson, who was a gunsmith at 244 High Street when a young man wearing a light overcoat came in. 'How much would a revolver cost?' he asked.

Porter replied, 'I'm sorry, I'm not the proprietor. Mr Hanson is out at the moment, but I expect him back later.'

'Have you any idea of the price of a revolver?'

'Well I'll have a look for you if you like.' But although Porter looked through Mr Hanson's stock of pistols he didn't see a price on any of them.

'It's not for me, it's for a friend in the country, you see. He wanted to know the price of a revolver.'

But the young man – it turned out to be Arthur Spencer of course – was to be disappointed. However he called at the shop again at about 9.50 p.m. that night. The shop was now closed but he went round to the side door and knocked. John Hanson had by this time returned home and had heard about the earlier visit. He opened the door and let his customer into his shop and Spencer eventually bought a six chambered revolver for 5s 6d and a box of fifty cartridges for 2s 6d. It turned out to be a very bad bargain, since the revolver was defective.

On Sunday evening Spencer again turned up at the Garner household. Once again he asked Mary to marry him and once again she refused. This time he produced the revolver. 'Look at this! I've bought a revolver. I'll shoot you and myself if you won't have me. I'll give you until Monday night to think about it.'

This put a different complexion on things. Was he serious or was he not? Mary was in two minds, so she decided to inform the police. As a consequence of this Police Sergeant Dawson called to see her at the house of a Mr Flear who lived nearby in Cross Street. She told the sergeant of Spencer's threat.

'What you will have to do, Mrs Garner, is to lay information against the man and take out a warrant with a view to having him bound over to keep the peace.' Mary thought about it.

'Will I have to go to court?' The policeman indicated that she would have to. 'I don't want to do that.' Like a lot of poor people at the time she had a fear of being involved with the law and was afraid of where it might lead. 'Can't you just have a word with him?'

P.C. Dawson told her that the proper procedures would have to be followed. And Mrs Garner changed her mind about it all. 'He won't do it you know. He's only doing it to frighten me. He wants me to take him back, but I don't intend to do so.' She wouldn't be budged, although the police tried to get her to take out a warrant for her protection. And finally she went away.

Whether Spencer did turn up on Monday night is not known, but he certainly came on Tuesday. At about 8.30 p.m. that evening Mrs Garner and her stepson John were sitting in the kitchen talking. The other three children were in bed, Ernest and Arthur in the same bed in the back bedroom and little Ada in her mother's bed in the front bedroom. Then somebody came and tried the back door which was locked.

'Who's there?' shouted Mary.

'It's only me, Arthur Spencer.'

'You'd better let him in,' said Mary to her stepson, and John unlocked the door. Spencer came in and sat down at the kitchen table.

'Have you got that popgun with you?' asked Mrs Garner.

'No I haven't.'

'I've been to the police you know. They know all about you having that gun.'

'I only showed it to you to frighten you. It isn't loaded.'

After some more discussion in which once again Spencer asked the inevitable question and received the inevitable answer he said he was going upstairs to fetch his box. Mrs Garner went next door to Mr Trollope to take him a pair of trousers she had been mending for him. When she got back Spencer called her from upstairs saying that he couldn't find some of his things. She mounted the stirs to go and help him.

John Garner sitting downstairs suddenly heard shots from upstairs. He jumped to his feet. But he was undecided what to do. Should he race upstairs to try and defend his mother as he guessed Spencer had shot at her? Or would the crazed butcher shoot him too? He raced next door shouting, 'He's shot mother!'

Ripon Street today, at the corner of Cross Street.

When he came back the house was full of the acrid smell of the powder from the discharge of the pistol. He heard someone stumbling down the stairs and rushed to see who it was. His mother, her front covered in blood, was leaning against the wall. 'Oh, Johnnie, come and help me.'

He raced upstairs and put his arm around his mother and helped her to stagger down the steps. He guided her through the kitchen and out into the back yard intending to get her into the house next door out of harms way. But she was losing consciousness and he propped her up against the window sill while he went to number 17 for assistance.

William Trollope, George Bassett, who lived across the street, and John Flear had all heard the shots and came rushing to 19 Stanley Place. They found Mrs Garner now in the kitchen lying in front of the fire. She had crawled there from the back yard. She was conscious by this time and when John Flear bent to examine her she said, 'Oh, my God. Save me for the sake of my children.'

They carried her into the Mr Trollope's house and sat her on a chair, but she passed out again. The men then told John Garner to fetch a doctor and the police and off the boy rushed. First he called at Surgeon Davidson's house nearby and told him where his mother was. Then he saw P.C. Revill in Canwick Road and told him about the shooting and the constable went to Mr Trollope's house while the boy went on to the police station.

The policeman found Mrs Garner sitting in a chair in the kitchen with her hat still on. Surgeon Davidson arrived and examined her, unfastening the broach which held her dress together at the top. He found a bullet which had entered her right breast and he told the policeman that he thought she was dying. P.C. Revill left her in the doctor's care and went next door. John Flear came with him. There was a light in the kitchen but the rest of the house was in darkness. Flear fetched a light and the policeman called upstairs, 'Arthur!' But there was no reply. P.C. Revill mounted the stairs cautiously. He found some blood on the door of the front bedroom but going into the room discovered, amazingly, a young child asleep in the bed. The back bedroom was different. It was full of smoke and reeked of powder. Arthur Spencer was lying on his back near the fireplace and a revolver lay near his feet. There were two young boys cowering in the bed.

P.C. Revill told Flear to take the boys and the young child in the other bedroom next door, and then bent to examine Spencer. He was alive but bleeding from the mouth. The policeman gave him a drink of water then had him moved to a small room over the scullery and placed on a bed there.

Meanwhile young John Garner had gone to the police station and came back with Inspector Briggs, who also called in Dr Harrison the police doctor. The inspector had Mrs Garner moved to a sofa and she died just after Dr Harrison arrived. It was discovered that she had been shot above the right breast. A second bullet was found when she was undressed but this had been deflected by her stays and had not injured her.

Arthur Spencer was found to have a wound in his mouth. He had first tried to shoot himself in the heart but the bullet had not penetrated his clothes, merely leaving a bruise above his heart. He had then fired the gun near his mouth which was blackened by the powder and he had a wound at the back of his throat. He was removed to hospital that night, but by the next evening he was well enough to ask the policeman sitting by his bed if Mrs Garner was dead. On being informed that she was he said, 'Oh dear. I shot her twice when she was on the landing going downstairs. It would not have occurred if she had taken the revolver from me on Sunday as I wanted her to. I had nowhere to keep it, only in my pocket.'

The jury at the inquest which was held in St Andrews School brought in a verdict of wilful murder against Arthur Spencer and the Lincoln City magistrates committed him for trial at the following Lincoln & Lincolnshire Assizes. On Saturday 11 July his trial opened before Mr Justice Vaughan Williams The prosecution was in the hands of Mr Appleton and Mr Bonner and Spencer was defended by Mr Lindsell. He could do little except to claim that Spencer's admissions should not be used in evidence, since he had not been cautioned that anything he said could be used in evidence. But the judge overruled him. The jury took only a quarter of an hour to bring in a guilty verdict and he was sentenced to death. And on 28 July at the Greetwell Road prison, Arthur Spencer, twenty-two and a pork butcher, was duly executed by James Berry.

10

Prolific Poisoner

Miss Emma Rowe stood and looked down at the body of her friend Mrs Maria Soames. Maria was lying in her bed and she looked peaceful now after all the pain and suffering she had been through. Emma took a lace handkerchief from her skirt pocket and dabbed her eyes. It was a Saturday, 18 October 1856, and Emma had finished her work for the week. She was a dressmaker and she worked from home. That is to say she worked from her lodgings at 27 Alfred Street, Bedford Square, London, and her landlady had been Mrs Soames. Emma had been there for some six years and she and Maria used to meet nearly every day in the large kitchen of the house and would chat. But about six weeks ago Mrs Soames seemed to have become much friendlier with another lodger in the house, Catherine Wilson.

Catherine Wilson was standing behind Emma as she gazed down at the features of her erstwhile friend. 'Would you come into my room for a moment, Miss Rowe? There's something I want to say to you.'

Emma followed the tall figure of Catherine into her room. In truth she was a little in awe of the rather dominating woman. At the beginning of Maria's short illness (she had only been taken ill on the Thursday before and she was dead on the Saturday), Catherine had told everyone that she had been a nurse and would look after Mrs Soames. She then told Emma that the doctor had informed her that Maria was to have as few visitors as possible and she asked Emma not to visit the sick woman. Then she said that, again on medical advice, she was to be the only one who could give the doctor's medication. Not even Maria's grown-up daughters who lived in the house would be allowed to give their mother her medicine. And she kept the two bottles of medicine locked up in her room.

Catherine looked down speculatively at Emma. 'Can you keep a secret?' she asked. Emma glanced up at her in rather a puzzled way but said that she could.

'Then I have something to tell you. But you must be careful not to say anything about it to anyone.' She paused for effect and gazed for a while at Emma. Then she said in a dramatic way, 'I believe that Mrs Soames' death was not a natural death.'

'What on earth do you mean?'

'I believe, well I'm sure of it, that Mrs Soames took something on that Thursday night, the night she was taken ill. She took it in brandy and water. I don't know what it was, but I believe she did it deliberately to do away with herself.'

'But why? Why would she want to kill herself?'

'She was tired of life. Don't you know about the man?'

'What man?'

Catherine shrugged her shoulders. 'She met this man. I don't know where or when, but she was besotted with him and he borrowed a lot of money from her. I think it was about eighty pounds. And he deceived her. She was very upset about it and I suppose she decided to end it all. And she took whatever it was, in my presence.' (£80 then would be worth over £50,000 today).

'But why did you allow her to do it? And why didn't you tell the doctor, or her daughters or her brother?'

'It's no business of mine what she did.'

'Well then. You must be the villain!'

Catherine said nothing to that.

Catherine Wilson was no stranger to death. In 1854 she was the house-keeper to a retired seaman in Boston. Peter Mawer was in his mid-fifties and suffered with gout. At that time a popular remedy to relieve the pain of the illness was colchicum. This was derived from the dried seeds of the meadow saffron, *Colchicum autumnale*, which grew in the fields in September. Powdered seeds could be added to an alcoholic drink, like brandy, and in very small doses, it did relieve pain. But five grams of the seeds are fatal to an adult. Colchicum is a cytotoxin or cell poison and its toxic action is very similar to arsenic. Hence it is often called 'vegetable arsenic'. The symptoms appear after a few hours and include burning in the mouth and throat, thirst, difficulty swallowing and frequent and violent vomiting. These last for twelve to twenty-four hours and then more serious symptoms develop, which are often mistaken for cholera, and the patient dies of paralysis of the central nervous system after another two days, or less if the dose taken has been large.

Scotland Yard.

Peter Mawer made a will leaving everything to Catherine Wilson in April 1854 and he died in October of the same year. His doctor put it down to him having taken a larger dose of colchicum than he was used to, to alleviate the pain, and unfortunately had accidentally taken too much. The seaman had a number of properties in the town and when these were sold Catherine Wilson inherited a substantial amount of money. She went off to London in November taking with her a newly acquired servant and soon met a man called James Dixon. They very quickly began a relationship and took lodgings with Mrs Soames, Catherine introducing Dixon as her brother. Then began a period of high and expensive living for the couple. Catherine bought jewels and dresses with gay abandon. But the money soon ran out and before Christmas the next year, Catherine was sending her servant, Elizabeth Hill, downstairs to borrow money from Maria Soames and sending the girl off to the pawn shop with her rings and dresses.

James Dixon was also being troublesome. He was a violent man when drunk, as he often was, and he beat Catherine brutally. But she had a remedy. She still had some colchicum seeds with her and soon Dixon fell ill and died. The doctor she called in, Dr Whidborne, was Mrs Soames' doctor but not Dixon's, and he refused to sign a death certificate without a post-mortem. This was duly performed but no poison was detected. Colchicum was extremely difficult to detect in those days and the symptoms were so like cholera that the death was often put down to that. At that time cholera was a very common cause of death in large cities.

At about this time Maria Soames inherited some money from the death of her father, although it didn't come in one lump sum. Her half-brother Samuel Barnes was the executor of her father's will and he gave money to Maria when she asked for it. Her husband had died a couple of years before, but with the rents from the several houses which she had acquired upon his death she was a comparatively wealthy widow. Catherine told Mrs Soames that she had been robbed in the street and had lost a substantial amount of money and she continually borrowed from her, sometimes receiving quite large sums. One loan was for £80.

It was in the October of 1856 when Mrs Soames died. Catherine, far from keeping what she had told Emma Rowe secret, had told practically everybody she met and Samuel Barnes, when he heard the rumours, became suspicious of his half-sister's death. He insisted that a post-mortem be done and an inquest be held. But again no poison was found in the body and Doctor Whidborne gave his opinion that death was due to natural causes. The inquest jury brought in a verdict to that effect.

Catherine Wilson moved back to Boston and took up lodgings with a Mrs Jackson. In 1859 Mrs Jackson died after a four day illness showing very similar symptoms to that shown by Mrs Soames, James Dixon and Peter Mawer. Mrs Jackson was also known to have had with her before her death £120. But after her death it could not be found. Suspicions were raised locally against Catherine and eventually the police began an investigation. Mrs Jackson's body was exhumed in January 1860, but no poison was found in the remains. The inquest jury again came to the conclusion that death had been by natural causes and the police investigation came to nothing.

Catherine rapidly moved away from Boston and took up lodgings in Loughborough Road, Brixton. She was shopping one day in 1860 when she made the acquaintance of a Mrs Atkinson. The woman had just lost her purse with all her money in it and Catherine sympathised, telling her that she too had lost hers some years before when it was stolen by a pickpocket. She offered to lend Mrs Atkinson some money so that she could get back home. Mrs Atkinson and her husband owned a millinery shop in Kirkby Lonsdale in Cumbria and she was grateful for the help that Catherine had given her. Catherine wrote to her several times pointing out the advantages of shopping in London and eventually Mrs Atkinson agreed to come to London and purchase stock for the shop. Catherine pointed out that it would be much cheaper for her to stay with her in Loughborough Road and offered to come round the shops with her to help with the purchases. Mrs Atkinson agreed and duly arrived to stay with Catherine. But her stay was short. Mr Atkinson received a telegram from Catherine telling him that his wife was seriously ill and imploring him to come immediately. But he was too late. By the time he arrived at Loughborough Road his wife was dead. Catherine knew that since the local doctor did not know the patient he would not give a death certificate immediately but would order a post-mortem on Mrs Atkinson. She therefore told the distraught husband that on her death bed Mrs Atkinson had beseeched her not to let the doctors cut up her body. In Victorian times the attitudes towards death were very different to what they are today. They had a horror of being accidentally buried alive and of the body being interfered with after death. Mr Atkinson readily agreed with his wife's apparent request and refused permission for an autopsy. But worse was to come for him. When he went through his wife's belongings after the funeral he found that nearly all the money she had brought with her for buying stock in London had disappeared.

'Oh, I'm terribly sorry,' said Catherine when Mr Atkinson questioned her about it. 'Didn't your wife telegraph you? She said she was going to. Apparently, she told me, she felt ill on the train coming to London and got off at Rugby. She fell asleep in the waiting room and while she was asleep her bag with the money in it was stolen. When she got here I had to give her money for the rent.'

'That was kind of you. But isn't that her ring you are wearing?'

'Oh, yes it is. She insisted on my having it for all the help I gave her.'

The Old Bailey.

But time was running out for Catherine Wilson, although it was to be another two years before nemesis finally struck. In February 1862 she was living with an old lady, Mrs Sarah Carnell in Crawford Street, Marylebone and acting as a nurse. Presumably she was hoping that the situation would be similar to that when she looked after Peter Mawer in Boston. She had persuaded the old lady to promise her a large legacy when she died, but she had by this time run out of colchicum seeds. When she was asked to collect the old lady's medicine from the chemist's shop she did so but brought back another bottle called 'black draught'. She told Mrs Carnell that it would be soothing for her and persuaded the old lady to take a drink while she was sitting up in bed. But Mrs Carnell quickly spat it out, complaining that it burnt her mouth. The spots of liquid on the bed sheets burnt holes in the bed clothes.

Catherine rushed out of the house and disappeared. But a few weeks later an observant policeman recognised her outside a railway station and arrested her. She was charged at Marylebone Police Court in April with having administered oil of vitriol (sulphuric acid) to Mrs Carnell with intent to kill her. She was committed for trial at the Central Criminal Court (the Old Bailey). The trial caused a sensation and was reported in all the newspapers of the day. But Catherine had a good lawyer. He argued that the administration was purely an accident. The chemists' assistant was inexperienced and simply gave Catherine the bottle of oil of vitriol by mistake. The judge however poured scorn on this suggestion saying that any dilution of the concentrated acid with water into another bottle would have rendered the bottle too hot to hold. But the jury were not convinced and gave Catherine the benefit of the doubt. She was found not guilty and discharged.

But the case had been followed by members of the Lincolnshire Constabulary. They informed the Metropolitan Police that they had evidence that she was implicated in several poisoning cases. And when Catherine Wilson stepped out of the doors of the Old Bailey she was rearrested. While she was in prison several bodies were exhumed, post-mortems redone and witnesses re-examined. In the end she was brought to trial at the Old Bailey on 22 September 1862 charged with the wilful murder of Mrs Maria Soames. But this time the big guns of the medical profession went into the attack for the prosecution. Dr Alfred Swains Taylor, Professor of Medical Jurisprudence at Guy's Hospital, and an acknowledged expert on poisoning, pointed out that that there was no possibility of discovering a vegetable irritant poison like colchicum in a body after burial. But he had studied carefully the case notes, listened carefully to the symptoms described in court and he was of the opinion that Mrs Soames died from large and repeated doses of colchicum. Dr Whidborne also now changed his opinion and agreed with Dr Taylor. Evidence was brought to show that Catherine administered all the medication Maria had taken, not allowing anyone else to give it to her and she kept it locked up in her room. Her constant borrowings from Mrs Soames, which were never repaid, were also brought to light. As was the fact that Mrs Soames was on the point of demanding some of the money back. The jury were finally convinced even though no direct evidence could be produced that she had administered the poison. The jury brought in a verdict of guilty. It is doubtful that Catherine would have got away from the law even if she had been found not guilty for other indictments for murder were pending against her. She was condemned to death. Catherine Wilson was hanged by William Calcraft outside Newgate Prison on 20 October 1862 before a crowd of 20,000 people. It was one of the last public executions of a woman.

II

A Fatal Passion

'Come into the front room and I'll show you my weddings presents,' said Mrs Edith D'Arcy. She was a widow and the licensee of the White Horse Hotel in Market Deeping and it was a Saturday night, 23 September 1922. With her were three young women. Two were her daughters, Ivy and Gertrude and the other was Evelyn Kitchener, the daughter of the man Mrs D'Arcy was due to marry in two days time. Evelyn and Gertrude had been to the pictures together and had returned to the pub at 9.15. They were met by Mrs D'Arcy and Ivy who invited them in to see the wedding presents laid out in the front room of the hotel.

Ivy, who was only two months short of her ninteenth birthday, had been married herself only three days before. It had been hoped that they could have had a double wedding, mother and daughter together, since Ivy was very close to her mother and indeed had worked all her life helping her mother in the hotel. She ran errands and helped out in the kitchen and later when she was old enough served in the bar. But it was not to be. Circumstances dictated otherwise. And Ivy married her boyfriend George Prentice, who worked for a barber in the village, on Wednesday 20 September, at St Guthlac's Church, just up the road from the White Horse.

'Gertrude. Bring the candle, dear. I won't bother to light the gas.' The four women came into the darkened room and Gertrude placed the candle on the big table in the middle of the room where the presents were laid out. They clustered round the table with Ivy standing next to her mother. Then Mrs D'Arcy picked up a present which had been given to her that very evening.

Suddenly there was the report of a gun, very loud in the confined space, a scream and the light went out. Mrs D'Arcy looked up at the door of the room where the sound of the shot had come from. And in the light cast by the passage behind she saw a figure standing in the doorway. She recognised him immediately as Frank Fowler, a farm worker from Langtoft, a village just up the road from Market Deeping. And he was carrying a gun, a double barrelled shotgun pointed at her. She was incredibly brave. She didn't hesitate. She ran at him – he was standing only three or four yards away from her – and grabbed the barrel of the gun. She wrenched the barrel up and the next shot went harmlessly out of the window.

Fowler swore at her and muttered, 'That one was for you!'

Fowler and Mrs D'Arcy wrestled for the gun. But the sound of the two shots and the scream had alerted customers in the bar and soon pounding feet heralded the presence of men from other parts of the hotel. Fowler was grabbed from behind by the customers while Mrs D'Arcy struggled to keep hold of the gun. When Fowler was eventually pulled away Mrs D'Arcy still grasped the gun and wouldn't let go. But Mr Alexander Ellis gently took hold of the barrel and

Contemporary view of the White Horse Hotel, Market Deeping.

said, 'Let me have the gun, Mrs D'Arcy,' and she eventually released her hold, panting, 'You be sure that you don't let Fowler have it!' Then Gertrude shouted,

'Bring a light. Ivy has been shot.' Mrs D'Arcy had some matches in the pocket of her apron and she lit the gas mantle. She saw Ivy now sitting in a chair. There was a terrible wound in her chest and she was covered in blood. She was clearly unconscious, her head leaning over sideways and if she hadn't been held upright by Gertrude and Evelyn she would have toppled out of the chair.

A few moments before, Evelyn had been standing next to Ivy, when she looked up and saw by the light of the candle Frank Fowler standing in the doorway. He had a gun pointed at Ivy. She heard the report and Ivy scream and then the light went out as the blast of the shotgun extinguished the flame. She immediately dropped to the floor and got under the table. She felt Ivy come down with her and thinking that she too was hiding she put her arms round her and then felt her clothes and hands getting wet. She and Gertrude managed to get the stricken young woman up and into a chair and then Mrs D'Arcy lit the gas.

A doctor was called but, while they waited, there was little that Mrs D'Arcy and her helpers could do for her daughter. And when Dr Benson arrived he pronounced Ivy Prentice dead. He afterwards reported that she had received the full charge from one of the barrels producing a wound almost three inches square. Several ribs were broken and she had died instantaneously as a result of haemorrhage and shock.

Before the doctor arrived several customers brought Fowler into the room to show him the damage he had done to Ivy. But all he said was, 'I have had my bloody revenge.' The police were fetched and Sergeant Bennett soon appeared at the White Horse Hotel. He took Fowler

St Guthlac's Church.

into custody and he reported that his prisoner said, 'I've done it sergeant. I will tell you all.' Fowler was taken to the police station in Market Deeping where he was charged with the murder of Mrs Ivy Prentice. He said, 'I have nothing to say now. If I had known I should not have been mixed up with a lot like them. It is their own fault.'

The inquest took place in a small room at the police station in Market Deeping on the following Monday. The inquest jury, as was the usual practice, were taken first to view the body which was laid out in the same room as the tragedy had happened. Afterwards they heard evidence that Fowler, who was thirty-five and worked on his aunt's farm at Langtoft, had been coming to the White Horse every Saturday night for several years. Mrs D'Arcy also said that her daughter Ivy, who was known in the pub as Polly, would often serve him and though she was a pleasant and cheerful girl, she paid him no more attention than she would any of her other customers. She certainly had never been out with him. And she had given him no cause for jealousy. Dr Benson also gave evidence and after the doctor had given his evidence the inquest was adjourned until the following Friday.

Mrs D'Arcy was married to William Kitchener, a railway signalman who came from Tallington, near Market Deeping, on the Monday the same day as the inquest. The ceremony took place at St Guthlac's and a large proportion of the population of the village attended in sympathy with the distraught mother.

The inquest was resumed the following Friday and the jury heard evidence from Evelyn Kitchener and from Gertrude D'Arcy. Gertrude described how, after the murder, she attacked Fowler who was being held by customers in the hotel and cried, 'Oh you devil! You've killed her!' and he replied, 'Yes. And I meant the other for your mother!'

William D'Arcy, who was the brother of the dead woman and also worked behind the bar, said that Fowler came into the hotel on the fatal Saturday night at about six o'clock. He talked to him for a few minutes but Fowler never mentioned Ivy. Fowler left the pub after about half an hour

The village of Langtoft just up the road from Market Deeping.

DOUBLE EXECUTION.

Fowler & Robinson Hanged at Lincoln.

George Robinson (27), and Frank Fowler 35), were executed at the County Prison, Lincoln, on Wednesday, the former for the murder of Francis Pacey at Dorrington, and he latter for the murder of Ivy Dora Prentice t Market Deeping.

About 160 people assembled outside he gaol, but beyond the tolling of the prison ell, there was nothing to indicate that the executions were being carried out,

Pierpoint, who arrived in Lincoln on Tuesay with an official from the Home Office, arried out the work quickly, the men being executed simultaneously.

The prisoners, since their sentence, had dopted an indifferent and somewhat callous titude, but it is understood they were more ubdued yesterday and attended to the nistrations of the Prison Chaplain, Canon cott. They walked firmly to the scaffold

A report from the *Louth Standard* for 16 December 1922.

but returned at nine o'clock and resumed drinking, but he had had only about three pints of beer over the whole evening. At a little after nine o'clock, Fowler left the bar and soon after that William D'Arcy heard two gunshots.

George Prentice, who had recently been married to Ivy D'Arcy, said that he had been on good terms with Fowler whom he had known for the last eighteen months, except for an occasion in March when he saw Fowler one evening in the White Horse. Prentice had been going out with Ivy for some time and Fowler knew about it. That night Fowler came up to him in the bar and said, 'I will have my own back on you one day.' Prentice was surprised because he had no idea that Fowler was fond of Ivy. At the end of the inquest the coroner summed up and the jury brought in a verdict of wilful murder against Fowler and he was committed for trial on a coroner's warrant.

Frank Fowler was brought before the magistrates at the Bourne Police Court on Thursday 12 October. The evidence given was much the same as at the inquest. Mrs D'Arcy (who was now Mrs Kitchener) described Fowler as being surly and morose. But this time Fowler was defended by Major Bell, a local solicitor. He suggested during his cross examination of her that it was well known that Fowler had an affection for Ivy. In fact he had been chaffed about wanting to marry her. But Mrs Kitchener hotly denied this.

Dr Benson also gave his evidence and when questioned about the mental state of Fowler said that as far as he knew he was perfectly normal. George Prentice said that at the time Fowler told him that he would have his own back one day, he was not actually engaged to Ivy. Thomas Day, who was a coal dealer in Market Deeping said that he was a regular customer at the White Horse and he had heard others kidding Fowler about Polly. They would say that Prentice was cutting Fowler out with regard to the young lady. And he heard Fowler say once in reply, 'It's all right, but it sticks in here,' pointing to his heart. On the night of the murder he afterwards asked Fowler, 'What made you do a thing like that?' And the man replied, 'I meant her mother too.' Fowler, through his solicitor, reserved his defence and was committed by the magistrates for trial at Lincoln Assizes on 31 October.

The trial opened before Mr Justice Lush and it was obvious that the defence would be insanity. His aunt was called and she said that her nephew had served in France during the war and had been badly affected by the experience. After he had been demobilised in 1919 he began to behave in peculiar ways. Sometimes he would swear at her for no reason and at other times begin to sing or recite poetry. He would complain that he was being followed and that when he was indoors people were looking in at him from the window. Early in September he had threatened to cut her throat. Doctors were also called by both sides to give evidence as to his mental state. But they gave conflicting stories. For the prosecution they came down on the side of normality and for the defence on the side of insanity. The judge's summing up was on the lines of there not being enough evidence to conclude insanity and the jury took the hint. After retiring for forty minutes they gave their verdict, guilty of murder. Fowler was asked if he had anything to say and he replied in an almost inaudible voice, 'Nothing, sir.' The judge then sentenced him to death.

The execution took place on Wednesday 13 December 1922 at the county prison on Greetwell Road in Lincoln and it was the first and only time that a double execution took place there. The other prisoner to be executed was George Robinson who was twenty-eight and had also been a serving soldier in the First World War. He lived in Dorrington, a small village near Sleaford, and he cut the throat of his girlfriend when she finally rejected him in September 1922, just a fortnight before Fowler committed his murder. They were hanged together by Thomas Pierrepoint, assisted by Robert Baxter. 160 people gathered outside the prison at the appointed time, eight o'clock in the morning, but apart from the tolling of the prison bell there was nothing to indicate that the executions were being carried out and the men, according to the Lincolnshire Chronicle, were 'plunged into eternity'.

A Humane Hangman

He was a man of middle height with a pale face, a narrow forehead and a fringe of dark whiskers. He was said to have restless eyes which never looked straight at anyone and he had thin cruel lips and a foxy smile. But this it must be said was an unflattering description by a newspaper reporter who did not approve of him. On this particular day he was travelling by train to Usk in Monmouthshire with the reporter who described him as wearing a rusty and threadbare black suit, with a watch chain over his waistcoat and a gem ring on his finger.

At a roadside station a young woman got in the carriage with a young child and he immediately made a fuss of the child. He took her on his knee and allowed her to play with his watch and chain and the ring on his finger. He produced peppermint lozenges from his pocket and put one in the child's mouth. He talked to the child's mother about the weather and the crops, prophesying that they would have a hard winter and lamented that working men often had to remain in poverty.

At Usk he left the carriage and walked quickly up the platform. The reporter assisted the young mother and her child out of the carriage and then informed her that the friendly gentleman she had been talking to was one of the most famous, or infamous, men in the country. He was William Marwood, the official chief hangman of Britain, and he had come to hang a young man of twenty now residing in Usk Jail!

William Marwood had been born in Goulceby, near Horncastle, in November 1818, the fifth of ten children. His father was a local boot and shoemaker, but young William was apprenticed to a local miller. Presumably with such a large family and because William was not the eldest boy, he could not be taken into the trade of his father. But young William was a clever and industrious lad and he eventually took up his father's trade. He was thirty-seven before he was able to set up his own business in Horncastle and six years later he got married. At the time he was living at 149 Foundry Street. His first wife died and he married again in 1867 when he was forty-nine. The marriage took place in the Wesleyan Chapel in Queens Street and soon after this he set up shop at 7 Church Lane opposite St Mary's Church. By this time he was a master shoemaker.

He had always been interested in the execution of felons by hanging. It was only in 1868 that hanging in public ceased. Before this it only took a trip to Lincoln on a market day (hangings were usually done on a market day to ensure a large crowd for the spectacle) and you could watch a hanging at Cobb Hall, the round tower at the corner of Lincoln Castle. Public hanging was a spectacle which offended a great many well known and influential people including Charles

William
Marwood.

Dickens. There would often be thousands present in an ill regulated and boisterous crowd with everything on sale from food and drink to ladies themselves, as depicted in the famous picture by Hogarth. With all this public interest in hanging it seems that Marwood himself had never witnessed a public hanging. But he was interested in the mechanics of the operation and felt, as many other people did, that it was a barbarous procedure. In the early days a rope was simply placed around the prisoner's neck and he or she was then pushed off a ladder or made to stand on a cart, which was then pulled away from beneath them. When gallows were used, as at Tyburn in London, prisoners were transported from Newgate to the place of execution by cart. They were not allowed to drink along the way and this gave rise to the saying 'on the wagon.' The gallows used in Calcraft's time (Marwood's predecessor) was not much better. A short drop left the victim hanging until he slowly strangled to death. If he had friends they might be allowed to pull on his legs to quicken the process or the hangman himself might perform the service for a consideration.

Marwood felt there must be a more humane way of doing it and he experimented with figures made from sacking and filled with straw until he developed his famous 'long drop' method. In this the noose was placed round the prisoner's neck so that the knot came under the ear. Then the length of the drop, which depended on the weight and build of the person to be hanged, was carefully calculated. When the trap door was opened the man fell through and the noose swung round jerking the head back and breaking the cervical column and causing almost instantaneous death. He then began the campaign to put his theories into practice. He wrote many letters to influential people protesting about the inhumanity of the methods in use and proposing his own as an alternative. It took years before it had an effect but eventually in 1871 he persuaded the governor of Lincoln Prison to let him come and explain his method. The governor was so impressed that the following year he allowed Marwood to carry out an execution. This was on William Henry Horry.

Marwood's shop in Church Lane.

Horry was the son of a brewer of Boston. He married in 1866 and he and his wife Jane ran an inn at Burslem in Staffordshire. But in March 1871 he sold the inn and on the proceeds began a roving life, sending his wife and three children to live with his father in Boston. He made Nottingham his base but visited his wife and family occasionally. But he became obsessed with the idea that his wife was unfaithful to him, although his fears were groundless. However with an obsession like this, the protestations of innocence are often seen as proof that the person is hiding something. He bought a revolver in Nottingham in January 1872 and a few days later arrived at his father's house in Boston and shot his wife dead. He was tried at the Lincoln Assizes on 13 March and sentenced to death by Mr Justice Quain.

The execution took place in Lincoln Castle on 1 April 1872. Marwood arrived at the prison in the castle the night before and observed the prisoner covertly. Then the prisoner was weighed and from this Marwood worked out the length of the drop. He hung sacks filled with sand on the end of his ropes overnight to stretch them and the next morning set up his scaffold in the castle yard. A contemporary report observed that 'the condemned man appeared perfectly resigned and walked with great firmness to the scaffold. When the bolt was drawn the culprit appeared to die instantly.'

Marwood was said to be kind to the prisoners he executed. 'I give the prisoners confidence,' he once said, 'by assuring them that I will not hurt them and that it would soon be over.' And he tried to be as quick as he could. He usually had an assistant who tied their legs together when they were standing on the trap door while he put a hood over their heads and adjusted the rope. Then at a word from Marwood the assistant stood clear while Marwood pulled the lever or drew the bolt which released the trap door.

Marwood believed implicitly in his work. He said at one point, 'I am doing God's work, according to divine command and the law of the British Crown.' But his occupation was not a popular one. And it was not unknown for a crowd to follow him when he left the prison after executing a young prisoner and hurl abuse, if nothing worse, at him. Newspapers were also

St Mary's Church, Horncastle.

sometimes not kind to him and the unflattering description given by a newspaper reporter at the beginning of this chapter is a case in point. The *Daily Telegraph* reported, 'It can be a matter of no public concern to know how Mr Marwood came to learn or to take up with his hideous trade…That any person not utterly hardened, depraved, and callous should seek to fill this wretched office is as inscrutable as it is disgusting.'

He was also not above criticism of his methods. A letter posted in London in September 1879 said, 'Subjoined is a list of criminals executed by Marwood, all of whom, according to the papers, showed signs of life, in a greater or less degree after the drop fell.' And there follows a list of thirteen prisoners executed in London (Newgate), Maidstone, Lancaster, Newcastle, Bristol, York and Liverpool (Kirkdale). But the writer concludes, 'In justice to Marwood it may be stated that in many cases criminals are described as dying instantaneously by his methods of execution; and instances are not wanting of a hard death by means of the short drop; e.g., that of Godwin, executed at Newgate on Whit Monday, 1874 – the last time Calcraft officiated there.'

At least William Marwood became popular in Horncastle. People would drop in to see him at his little shop in Church Lane for a chat or just to see the famous personality who travelled all over the country. And he did. He travelled to all parts of England, Scotland and Wales and even to Ireland. In his eleven years as a hangman he is estimated to have executed over 350 men and women, including Charles Peace who became one of the most famous criminals in England. He was paid £10 for each execution (over £630 in today's money) and he received 50d in expenses for each journey. But it must have been exhausting work, travelling up and down the country, mostly on trains and eating scratch meals when and where he could.

And the exhaustion may have told on him. Certainly his last execution was one of the most dramatic. It concerned James Burton, who was thirty-three years old and had murdered Elizabeth Sharpe at Tunstall, near Sunderland on 8 May 1883. He made a full confession of his crime in a letter he wrote to the woman's parents. In the letter he says that they had a quarrel while they were walking up a lane at Tunstall. He put out a hand to give her a note she had dropped, when according to him, she screamed and poked him in the chest with her umbrella. She then threatened to call her brother who she said would deal with him severely and again poked him with her umbrella. Then he claims that he lost his temper and hit her and they both fell to the ground. She got up first and cried out, 'Oh Jim Burton! I'm only trying you. Don't hit me anymore.'

'But,' he wrote, 'I said, "It's too late now, for I have not a home for myself!" I was blind with passion and I picked up a stone and hit her with it and she fell down. Then after I had seen what I had done I placed the stones that were lying around on top of her.' He then described how he watched the scene until he saw her body discovered by some railway men. He expressed much penitence for the crime.

On the morning of Monday 5 August within the walls of Durham Gaol, James Burton rose at 7 a.m. and was joined by the prison chaplain. In the press-room he complained that Marwood had pinioned him too tightly, but Marwood said that it would be better for him like that. As they walked to the scaffold Marwood kept a tight hold of the buckle of the strap in the centre of the prisoner's back. The executioner, the prisoner, the chaplain, the sheriff's bailiff, the chief warder and two other warders went up the steps of the scaffold. The prison surgeon, and the governor, the undersheriff, three reporters and several other warders stood about 100 yards away. Marwood at once set about adjusting the noose, putting the prisoner with his back to the lever and allowing a drop of seven and a half feet.

The prisoner could be heard by the distant spectators praying with the chaplain and he was giving a response just as Marwood put his hand on the lever. A warder put his hand on Marwood's arm and the executioner waited. The chaplain had just said the words, 'Lord, receive the soul of this man about to die,' And the prisoner had replied, when Marwood raised the lever. There was a bang as the trap swung open and the man disappeared into the cavity. But immediately it was apparent something was wrong. The rope was seen to swing about wildly. One of the warders caught it and swung it over to Marwood who had rushed round to the side of the trap. With the aid of another warder he pulled the man up until he appeared to be sitting on the edge of the trap. It was then found that the slack of the rope had caught under the man's right elbow as he fell thus relieving the pressure on his neck. Marwood however quickly adjusted the slack of the rope to its proper position and readjusted the white cap which had slipped up and as the two warders relinquished their grip on the man he was sent into the cavity again.

The man was cut down after an hour and the usual inquest was held. The chief warder and the sheriff's officer both gave evidence and stated that Marwood was sober and performed his work as usual. Marwood was called and he explained that the prisoner had fainted just as he was raising the lever and falling over sideways had caused the rope to become tangled under his arm. He said that the accident might be avoided in future by a couple of planks being placed across the cavity and two warders standing by to support the prisoner if necessary. The jury returned the usual verdict.

A fortnight later William Marwood died of pneumonia at his home in 64 Foundry Street. It was 4 September 1883 and he was sixty-three years of age. He was buried in the graveyard of the Holy Trinity Chapel on Spilsby road, but within a short time souvenir hunters had torn pieces off the grave stone and it was removed. He now lies in an unmarked grave. But a plaque outside his little shop in Church Lane (it's now a private house) celebrates his life and he is remembered by a children's rhyme of the time:

If Pa killed Ma,
Who'd kill Pa?
Marwood.